THE CHOICE

THE CHOICE

POLAND, 1939–1945

Irene Eber

SCHOCKEN BOOKS

NEW YORK

All rights reserved under International and Pan-American Copyright
Conventions. Published in the United States by Schocken Books, a division
of Random House, Inc., New York, and simultaneously in Canada
by Random House of Canada Limited, Toronto. Distributed by
Pantheon Books, a division of Random House, Inc., New York.

Schocken and colophon are registered trademarks of Random House, Inc.

Chinese names and terms are transliterated in accordance
with the Pinyin system.

Library of Congress Cataloging-in-Publication Data

Eber, Irene [date]
The choice : Poland, 1939–1945 / Irene Eber.
p.   cm.
Includes index.
ISBN 0-8052-4197-3 (hardcover)
1. Eber, Irene.   2. Jews—Poland—Mielec—Biography.   3. Holocaust,
Jewish—Poland—Mielec—Personal narratives.   4. Mielec (Poland)—
Biography.   I. Title.

DS135.P63E234 2004   940.53'18'092—dc22   [B]   2003067353

www.schocken.com

Book design by M. Kristen Bearse
Map by Jeffrey L. Ward

Printed in the United States of America
First Edition
2   4   6   8   9   7   5   3   1

For my beloved family—
Jonathan Michael and Miriam Alisa Eber
Lore and Susan Ann Smith
Sandra Naomi and Michael Lynn McDowell

And to the memory of the Geminder and Ganger family
members who perished in World War II—
My father, Yedidia Geminder
His sister Sheindl Padawer
Her children, Hella and Gerda
His sister Feige Kurtz
Her husband, Reuven Kurtz
Their children, Malka and Esther
My mother's sister Hanna Lipper
Her husband, Leo Lipper
Their son, Heini
Her sister Dora Kalman
Her husband, Julius Kalman
Their children, Evelyn and Horst
Her sister Clara Riesel's children, Püppe (Friedel), Ette (Senta), and Heinz

CONTENTS

Baltic Sea

Gdańsk

POLAND

Wisła R.

Bug R.

BELARUS

Warszawa (Warsaw)

Łodz

Parczew
Włodawa
Sosnowice
Lublin
Sobibór
Bełżyce
Trawniki
Piaski
Izbica

0 Miles   50   100
0 Kilometers   100

Wisła R.

Czermin   Cyranka
Radomyśl Wielki   Mielec
Kraków   Dębica

Bełżec

Lwow

Wisłoka R.

CZECH
REP.

UKRAINE

North
Sea

Baltic Sea

Berlin
Halle
Warsaw
POLAND
Leipzig
GERMANY
Mielec

0 Miles   200   400
0 Kilometers   400

Jeffrey L. Ward

THE CHOICE

CHAPTER ONE

≡≡≡

FIRST JOURNEYS

*In mid-March 1942 some 75 to 80 percent of all victims of the
Holocaust were still alive, while 20 to 25 percent had perished. A
mere eleven months later, in mid-February 1943, the percentages
were exactly the reverse. At the core of the Holocaust was a short,
intense wave of mass murder.*

CHRISTOPHER R. BROWNING, *Ordinary Men*

One day Father stopped singing. I can't remember if it was
shortly before the end—the death and destruction of Jewish Mielec—or if it was even earlier. Father loved music. He sang
to me, to himself, to anyone who would or would not listen. And
while his songs were probably no longer as happy once the Germans came, he had continued to sing the Yiddish tunes of which
he knew an astonishing number. "Zion, in the green fields," sang
Father, "where lambs pasture . . ." At his death Father was fifty-
one years old. Had he lived longer, I wonder how I would remember him. Would he still seem as joyful, a singer of songs only he
seemed to know? I didn't hear of Father's death until much later,
and at the time I had not learned how to mourn.

I remember how Mielec ceased to exist. The day it started to
disappear and the week that followed are as clear for me today as
ever. Since that first day I live and relive the events, again and
again, in dreams and in waking. As in a silent movie, scenes

appear and fade away; faces emerge, are captured, and vanish; silent shapes trudge across an endless frozen landscape and I am an actor in the fearful drama, playing my part, one of the crowd.

I can recall vistas and scenes of the town as it had been once. I see its unpaved broad and narrow streets, neatly laid out around the two cobblestoned markets, one large, the other small, both muddy in fall but sparkling with pure white snow in the wintry sun. From the window above Grandmother's store, I look down into Sandomierska Street, where something interesting always happens. It might be a wagon stuck in the mud, or a farmer driving his sleigh to market, unaware that the town urchins have tied their sleds to it and are hitching a ride. It might be the rebbe's hugely overweight wife sitting, in summer, in front of her house surrounded by her children of all ages and sizes, twelve of them, or fifteen. Cousin Esther and I play at guessing which is the youngest and which the oldest, or which two might be twins. But it is hard to tell any of them apart; they look so alike. Or it might be a father spanking his howling son for some misdeed. I like watching the street from above, especially the covered passageways that lead from the houses surrounding the Large Market to the street in back of it. From the apartments above they look like the mouths of dark tunnels from which people emerge and into which they disappear, disappear and emerge, are swallowed up and spat out. But soon I stand again in the marketplace, one of perhaps as many as eight thousand Jews, and together with them I am marched out of town along the hard, frozen road that cuts diagonally across the Large Market.

How trustworthy is my memory? I ask myself today. Is that how the end of Mielec, a small town in western Poland, began? Of course, to a participant and to an observer the event remembered is only the fragment witnessed, never the whole event in all its complexity. After all, the actor in a play remembers only his part and not those of others; the blind Indian describes the elephant as the trunk that his hand touches; the Chinese philosopher's well frog thinks the round piece of sky above the well is the world. The story I am about to tell is only a fragment, yet I know that even if it is a small portion of history regained, other fragments of history will in turn be lost.

Each winter, there were nights when the muddy streets froze and the marks left in the mud by the horses' hoofs and the peasants' wagons turned into uneven, stonelike indentations. Some days gray clouds enveloped the frozen landscape. Then it began to snow for days on end and beautiful ice flowers sprouted on the windowpanes. But this third winter of the war was different. Except for a few insignificant flurries at the beginning of winter, snow was not plentiful until later; the air was dry and cold, without even enough moisture for icicles to form along the roofs.

The rhythm of the town's life continued that winter—Thursday market days, daily searches for food, Germans catching Jewish men for work, Jews being beaten and having their beards shaved—but beneath these regularized routines, as frightening as they were, there was also a particular tension, a disquiet, fueled by rumors of what the Germans planned to do next. I believe the rumors began in December 1941, and by the middle of January the facts were known: The Jews from Mielec were to be deported. At first a figure of two thousand was mentioned, then forty-five hundred. But there were surely more than forty-five hundred Jews in Mielec by 1941, after refugees had begun pouring in, deported from other areas by the Germans. So what was in store for the many thousands aside from those who were to be sent "east," to the Lublin district? We would soon find out—there would be selections and killings. Meanwhile, even though ever since the

Germans had come Jews had been driven about like so many cattle from one town to another, had been locked into ghettos, dragged off to work camps, we knew this deportation would be different. Until then in no town had the entire Jewish population been deported. But that winter we were about to become pioneers in the experience of total deportation. Who could have known then (as I have learned since) that Mielec was singled out for this distinction by the newly created Operation Reinhard. When history came to be written, Mielec went on record as being the first *Judenfrei* town in the General Government of Poland.

How the information of our impending deportation filtered down to us is somewhat of a mystery. The German order was apparently leaked in Lublin and traveled 150 miles westward, even though only the Germans had telephones, and it was soon common knowledge in Mielec. The Germans were not pleased.

From a letter dated January 20, 1942:

To the Authorities of the General Government, Kraków
Re: Jewish Resettlement in the Districts Chełmno and Hrubieszów
   Although it is clear that the head of the Jewish Aid Committee for the Lublin District already knew on January 18 of the letter that had arrived on January 17 which ordered the above resettlement of Jews, in checking with my aide, I can inform you that it seems impossible that he [the Jew] would have learned [of the letter's contents] from someone employed here. It is possible that the Jew in question overheard a telephone conversation from the hallway. . . .

Soon there were new rumors. The threatened deportation was to be postponed, or the order might be rescinded, provided the Jews delivered all gold, jewelry, furs, and other valuables to the Germans. Did the Judenrat, the Jewish Council, intend to bribe the Germans with necklaces and rings? Or was this the Germans' idea—having the Jews deliver their valuables voluntarily so that they did not have to search for them?

Mother took out her jewelry box, that magic box she opened sometimes just for me, allowing me, under her watchful eye, to carefully handle the rings with their sparkling stones, and the heavy gold necklaces with their intricate patterns that caught the light when held just the right way. Most of all, I loved the strings of pearls, so cool and hard to the touch, yet suffused with an inner warmth. Now that our very existence was said to depend on it, Mother selected pieces to take to the Judenrat, but she decided to keep her dearest possession, Great-grandmother Blime's pearls, the ones that had adorned her turban when she was alive. The pearls, a few necklaces, a ring or two, Mother's Persian lamb and silver fox (the glass eyes looking as real as ever), and a few photographs were taken to Korpantowa, a Polish woman the family had known for many years, for safekeeping in case the bribe was ineffective. As Mother carried her jewelry to the Judenrat she believed, no doubt, with one half of her heart, that she was doing her part to save us and the Mielec Jews.

The other half of her heart told her not to trust the Germans' (or the Judenrat's) promises. We began to pack. In every Jewish house people packed—bundles, suitcases, big bags, small ones, nothing too heavy, for we had also to carry food. Long discussions ensued about what to take, what to discard; bags were packed and repacked. Summer clothes were needed, for eventually summer would come, but winter clothes were bulky, leaving no room for lighter items. My backpack was small and Mother told me to wear several dresses, one over the other. She laid these out on a chair, telling me not to forget them—there might be confusion when we had to leave.

At last we were ready. The bags were packed and stood neatly lined up in front of the attic door of the small room where I lived with my parents, my sister Lore, and Cousin Püppe. Now the room was even more crowded than usual, and someone was forever stumbling over the bags. Mother's final act in preparing for the journey was to sew some dollar bills (where and when she got them, I'll never know) into the hem of her checkered winter coat. They were crisp and new and Mother immediately worried that their rustling could be heard.

And then we waited. We began a strange existence in which every activity, all daily work, revolved around the question of whether we would or would not be here tomorrow, or the day after. I was told to stay close to home; if the order to leave came, others would not have time to look for me. Overnight our home had lost its permanency; it had become a strange place, a mere way station. Familiar objects lost their warmth. Nerves were taut. We sniped at each other. Electricity was in the air, like before a storm. When I look back at those weeks when we waited, not with hope that we would be somehow saved, but resigned to the inevitability of having to leave the place we called home, I am amazed. How was it possible that we so readily resigned ourselves to this unreal situation? After all these years I still cannot understand how quickly we accepted losing control of our lives. We waited.

I went to see my best friend, Tośka, who lived with her mother and sister at the Small Market. The three of them were waiting too, seated around their table in the gray afternoon light, the lamp unlit, not uttering a word. They invited me to sit with them, and I was reminded of a wake Tośka and I had read about. Afterward I walked through the nearly deserted streets to see my cousin Esther, finding things not much better there. Uncle Reuven was not at home; as a member of the Judenrat he was always at meetings during these days of waiting. Cousin Esther and her older sister, Malka, sat huddled next to the stove in the upstairs room. They too were silent. I may have asked Cousin Esther what she thought would happen, and she probably sneered at me in the condescending way she had, as if to say only fools would believe in miracles. I was twelve years old, and Cousin Esther was only two years older than I, yet since the Germans had come she seemed to have changed. She was no longer a child. Her mother, my aunt Feige, was in the store below, restlessly shifting the few meager stocks of food from one place to another. She no longer had much to sell; her supplies had dwindled since the war had started, and there was no point in even trying to get supplies if any day now everything would be left behind.

Days went by and soon they lengthened into one week and then another. Tiny flames of hope were kindled and, cautiously at first, we resumed our daily routine. One by one, we took articles of clothing we could not do without out of the bags. Mother moved the bags to the attic. Gradually her customers reappeared, to have her type petitions for travel permits. Maybe in another few weeks, they said, the storm will blow over.

It all happened so long ago that I cannot vouch for the extent of our information then, or how much hope, the handmaiden of illusion, influenced everyone's perceptions. Even so, there are some matters I know today that no one could have known then, not even Uncle Reuven, who as a Judenrat member was better informed than other people. I know now that the Mielec *Aktion* had merely been postponed. The deportation order was never rescinded, and the valuables delivered to the Judenrat had bought nothing for the Jews of Mielec but time, for waiting. I also know now that the Germans had already decided on our destination in January. We were to be sent to towns close to Bełżec, Chełmno, and Sobibór, the death camps. All this I can read today in the documents.

From a telegram dated January 21, 1942:

To the Authorities of the General Government, Kraków
Personally to Major Ragger
Re: Evacuation of Jews from Mielec
    The telegram from 6 January concerning the resettlement of 2,000
Jews is superseded. New number is 4,500. Distribution planned
as follows: 1,000 Radzyń district; 500 Zamość district; 1,500 Hru-
bieszów district; 1,500 Chełmno district.

And I know today that Uncle Reuven was taken as much by
surprise as we were when waiting came to an end on March 9. The
German order was given by telephone on Saturday, March 7, at
1:30 p.m., no doubt after a hearty midday meal.

I have retained the following memory of March 8: Heavy
pounding boots are heard on the staircase. They approach our
tiny, crowded room, the door flies open, and suddenly huge, gray-
coated men seem to fill every inch of space in that little room; they
seem to breathe all the air there is. We shrink from them into the
corners. Their brutal red faces tower above us, among them that
of the hated Rudi Zimmermann, an old family friend who was
now a *Volksdeutscher,* a member of the Gestapo, and a killer. Neither they nor we utter a word; no words are needed, our lives are
in their hands. But no, they did not come to kill. Zimmermann
merely takes Mother's typewriter and they march out the door.
We hear their boots pounding down the staircase. After a long,
agonized silence, fear hovering in the airless room more palpably
than ever, Mother whispers that she understands. Tomorrow we
will be deported, she says, her face white as a sheet. They've taken
the typewriter because petitions to travel are no longer needed.

Suddenly we were galvanized into action. We retrieved the suitcases from the attic, packing frantically, helter-skelter, now with-

out forethought or plan. Dresses were stuffed into the bags, taken out again, exchanged for others. Underwear was pulled out of drawers, examined, thrown on the floor. Slabs of Mrs. Feiner's heavy bread were brought from the kitchen and piled on the bed, there being no room anywhere else. Within no time at all, the little room was transformed into bedlam.

I felt like a stranger in that room, already homeless, for home had ceased to be the warm, familiar place I knew. Not knowing what was in store for us, surrounded by chaos, I was wholly preoccupied with this new condition of homelessness. It needed to be understood, gotten used to. I thought of the pitiful rabbi's wife without eyelashes (so different from our own rebbe's fat wife)—she and her two whining children who had come to Mielec the year before as refugees. They lived with Mrs. Feiner, who baked bread for a living, but this was not their home; they too were homeless. I felt guilty for disliking the woman and her children now that we were about to be refugees ourselves in an unknown place. It did not occur to me (for there was no way anyone could know) how close to death rather than only homelessness we were.

In the summer when war broke out, refugees had swarmed through the streets begging for bread and milk. Would we have to beg where we were going? Even if precious little bread and milk were now available in Mielec, maybe neither was to be had where we were going and no amount of begging would fill our stomachs. Fear of the unknown overwhelmed me and I could tell no one about it; my father, mother, sister, even loud Cousin Püppe (who lived with us after her parents had died), were as panic stricken as I, finding an outlet only in frantic packing and unpacking. Each of us was trapped on an island of silent terror.

Travelers leaving on a journey often take a long, last look at the home they are about to leave. An image of the rooms, their furnishings, pictures on the walls, fabrics on chairs, all the little useful

and useless items that make life comfortable imprint themselves
on the mind. Images of home will be taken along by the travelers
until they return again to their familiar surroundings. For us,
when the gray morning dawned, there was no time for leavetak-
ing. We knew we would never return anyway, and we knew that as
soon as we were gone, the landlord and his hard-faced, bony wife
would carry off our possessions one by one.

The next morning—a Monday—all of the Jews of Mielec were
collected in the Large Market amid shouts and shooting. There
were selections (this was made clear to me only many years later
from photographs taken by a German): Young men were lined
up—we didn't know for what purpose at the time—old men were
taken away, their bundles left behind in a pile. And others, we
among them, were soon driven like an enormous herd of cattle
along the road that cuts diagonally across the Large Market. Eyes
behind lace curtains, half-concealed faces behind closed windows,
silently watched the moving, seething, running, stumbling dark-
clad mass of people, urged on by Germans who blindly hit us and
shot into the mass, pulled out men and women, lining them up in
a field to be shot when Mielec had receded in the distance for the
rest of us. How many died that morning in the field, killed by men
turned monsters, I shall never know.

I am back in Mielec. It is September 1980. I ask to be driven
along this road, the road to Berdechow, the endless road of suffering that had been drenched in blood. In vain I hope to see a
mass grave, a burial place of the old, the sick, and the feeble who
were shot along the way when they could run no longer. There is
none. Now, I speed along on the road to Berdechow in comfort.
Then, we ran and stumbled along this road, deaf to everything
except the German shouts, gunfire, the screams of the wounded

and dying. We ran in fear for our lives, clinging to one another lest we lose sight of each other, not knowing who would be next to fall, to lose his life, to be pulled out of the running, stumbling mass and singled out for murder. Silent fields stretch into the distance, along both sides of the road to Berdechow, just as they did then—the silent earth, grave of so many. Who mourns for them now? I wonder. I want to ask the driver if farmers ever find bones when they plow their fields, but he is not from these parts and wouldn't know. The thousands of people who trod on this road have left no mark.

The car covers the few miles quickly. Then, I remember, the hard, frozen road seemed to go on forever. I try to remember how long this death march lasted, but I can't. Time was suspended then, had become meaningless. For what can be the meaning of time when death is that close and when fear, the fear of stumbling and falling, the fear of a German bullet, is the only reality there is?

In a history book the fate of the Mielec Jews merits a brief, inaccurate paragraph: ". . . the action was carried out, with marked brutality and cruelty, from March 7 to 9. Large numbers of Jews were shot on the streets of the town, and in the airfield nearby. The remaining Jews . . . were deported to different localities in the Lublin district." The historian does not know that the *Aktion* lasted only one day, nor is he able to describe what death and fear of death are like. But I cannot blame him. History must be based on facts. Evidence is lacking for what really happened on that day in March 1942, except for what I or someone else who was there sometimes clearly, sometimes dimly, remembers. Exactly what transpired—how many were killed, how many were selected for work camps, how many were shipped east—is preserved only as remembered fragments. Each of us who stood that day in the marketplace and marched on the road to Berdechow and survived has different fragments; those who oversaw the deportation or carried out the killings would rather not remember that day at all. Yet there was at least one German, charged with observing the events, who twenty years later did remember being told by one of the participants that the men who carried out the *Aktion* were "intoxicated by blood" ("*in einem Blutrausch*").

After the expulsion from Mielec and the march of terror and death I measured time as hunger, thirst, and fear of being killed. We were marched to the airfield some miles out of town and herded into aircraft hangars. Even after the killings, and after many men were selected for work camps, we still numbered several thousand people. Settled on the hangar floor I began to cry uncontrollably. Mother and Father tried to comfort me—what comfort was there?—but I remember crying a very long time. When at last I ran out of tears, I went to look for relatives Esther, Malka and Aunt Feige, and friends Tośka, her mother and sister.

People were packed tightly in the huge hangar, as far as the eye could see, sitting or standing in the dim recesses. Families were camped out on the floor as if for a macabre picnic. Parents hugged their children, old men prayed, infants cried, mothers shrilly called to older children, others simply stared vacantly, or wrinkled their brows in concentration as if trying to figure out where they were, or how they got to be in this place. An incessant babble of voices filled the hangar. Faces seemed to float by and disappear as I stumbled over children and bundles.

No matter how hard I looked, not a single familiar face emerged from the closely huddling groups of people. The more I looked the more the people merged into one, an undifferentiated gray-black mass. There seemed to be no one I knew, no one who knew me. They seemed oblivious even to my climbing all over them and stepping on their belongings. It was as if all of us, having lost our homes, had also lost our identities, lost whatever made us recognizable to one another. I became frantic. Sometimes I thought I saw a familiar profile— Tośka's delicate shape, Esther's stringy hair—but when I approached, trampling over people and bundles, the person turned out to be a stranger. Who are these people? I asked myself. They must be from elsewhere, they can't be from Mielec. Are all the people from Mielec dead, killed on the road to Berdechow? I became disoriented among these strangers.

Panic-stricken, I made my way back. Suddenly I was not sure whether I would find my little family alive. In a world gone mad where the known had ceased, I searched frantically for our small circle on the cold hangar floor. After I had found them, I sat close to my family and looked at their faces, the only familiar faces in this new world. Convinced that everyone else I had ever known in Mielec was dead, I did not again leave Mother's side.

We received neither food nor water. Slowly and sparingly we ate whatever we had brought. We melted the snow we found around the hangar for drinking water. We discovered that snow water does not quench thirst, so we used it mainly to wet our parched lips and mouths. The snow soon disappeared or was trampled to slush by the careless people.

Long ditches had been dug next to the hangar, and boards had been put on two stands, one at each end of the ditches. These were the "toilets." Men and women sat under the watchful eyes of the guards, exchanging information and conjectures about our ultimate fate. From the German point of view, the toilet was probably further proof of our subhuman nature. At one point during our time in the hangar, Mother decided to destroy the dollars she so carefully had sewn into the hem of her checkered coat. It didn't seem strange to me then, and only does so now, that she thought if the dollars were discovered we would be killed for having foreign money. We went to the "toilet," tore the crisp bills into tiny pieces, and dropped them into the stinking ditch. It was obvious to her as well as to me then that our lives depended on not having this money. Today I interpret this episode symbolically: It meant that we still had some control over life and death, that we could still make decisions, that we controlled our destinies. It was an illusion, of course. And had we kept the dollars we could have put them to good use later that summer.

After a day or so, our safe little circle became home, the babble of voices, the camping out a seemingly normal form of existence. In spite of gnawing hunger and parching thirst, it gradually came to seem as if at one time or another it was everyone's fate to live on hangar floors, never changing clothes or washing. If we ever had a home where we slept in beds, it was long ago, in a barely remembered past.

One day, a train was brought to a siding nearby—it was a steaming locomotive with a long row of cattle cars—and with much shouting and many beatings (even they no longer seemed extraordinary) most of the hangar dwellers were loaded onto the train. Packed tightly into the cattle cars, with not enough room for everyone to sit, we held on to the little food we had left. The small window afforded only a smidgen of light and air. Now the hangar seemed like paradise lost. While there, we at least had been close to Mielec, we had air to breathe, space to move in. Now the world had shrunk to a conveyance on wheels that was about to take us to a place we had never seen or heard of. Exhausted by hunger and thirst, I did not ask where the train was taking us. All that mattered now was to remain alive until the end of this journey.

Once again time lost its meaning. The train moved occasionally. Often it stood still on sidings. There were brief moments at the window for gasps of air, unheard pleas for water, and finally silent stupor when no one cared any longer how far we had traveled or where we were. Life as it once was lived in Mielec and even in the hangar receded into a past as unreal as the present. There was only the terrible thirst, the twilight inside a cattle car in motion with its befouled, stinking human cargo. Stripped of all identifying marks of our former station in life, we deluded human beings nonetheless still believed that the journey's end would restore us to some form of acceptable life. Rich and poor, young and old, good and bad, honest and crooked, had been reduced to one common goal: to stay alive until arrival.

From a telegram dated March 10, 1942:

Urgent—Submit Immediately—Strictly Confidential
Governor of the Lublin District, Inner Administration
Re: Evacuation of Jews from Mielec
   March 11 a transport of 2,000 Jews from Mielec will leave for final destinations Parczew and Międzyrzec. At both destinations 1,000 Jews will be unloaded. Arrival in Parczew, March 12, 5:53 a.m. . . . Arrival in Międzyrzec, March 12, 12 o'clock noon.

One evening we arrived in a snow-covered town, its roofs sparkling under a bright moon. Not a soul could be seen, though it surely must have been a substantial town since it had a railway station. We were quickly unloaded and driven into a large building for the night. That the building was pitch-dark did not matter; we were exhausted and simply collapsed on the cold floor. We had no need of light, nor the strength for curiosity to wonder what this building was, or into which town we had been disgorged. It was no longer important. We were too exhausted even to ask why there were so few of us now, thousands less than had been on the road to Berdechow. I wasn't even afraid—fear requires energy and I no longer had the strength to be afraid. I slept.

The next morning we were driven outside by the German soldiers. It was a bright, sunny, and incredibly cold day. A dazzling white blanket of snow covered the fields as far as the eye could see. Not a soul was about; the streets were deserted. Once again, a long column of people dressed in black formed under the Germans' watchful eyes. It wended its way like a giant dark snake out of the snow-covered town into the white countryside. But this time the march to an unknown destination was different. On the road to Berdechow people had darted every which way in wild confusion, dodging the Germans' blows and bullets. Now, sapped of energy, we trudged along, intent on each step, careful not to lose our footing on treacherous, slippery icy stretches.

I don't remember seeing villages along this road; there was no one to look at us from behind closed windows. Nor do I recall seeing anyone else on this deserted road that stretched far into the distance in an eerily silent and empty landscape. I saw neither farmers driving their sleighs to market nor women walking from one village to another. On this day, none but the Mielec Jews and the Germans in their sleighs with their guns and dogs were on the road. And only the Germans knew where it led.

From a letter dated March 18, 1942:

To the Governor of the District Department of Inner Administration, Population and Welfare, Lublin
Re: Transfer of 1,000 Jews; Destination Railroad Station Parczew
As I already informed you by telephone, the transport arrived in Parczew March 13, 1942. The police on the train [destined for Chełmno] relate in this connection the following: "On 13.3.42 in the evening toward 17:00 o'clock, a transport of 1,000 Jews was received in Parczew by the police. Their [the Jews'] continued dispatch occurred 14.3.42. Of the Jews, 200 were housed in Sosnowice and 800 in Włodawa. There were no difficulties during shipping.

Once more a different kind of time took over, no longer the timeless, endless time of a moving and stopping train. Every minute was precious on this road, each second marked by the nearness of a bullet or a fatal blow. Every step we took without falling, aware of having strength for yet another, meant going on living for a moment longer, though how long was in no one's power to know. Our march was not noisy, not in the way it had been on the road to Berdechow. No one had strength left for talking; our mouths were parched with thirst. Even the Germans, perhaps responding to the awesome whiteness surrounding us, were less boisterous and shouted less. But there were other sounds: the cracking of whips on horses' hides and human bodies, and, at regular intervals, single shots in back or ahead of us.

Those who slipped and fell, or fell from exhaustion and could not get up, were killed on the spot. There were others who had apparently reached the end of their strength, or who had perhaps concluded that having lost control over their lives, they should, at least, retain control over their dying. Men and women dropped out of the dark column, walked to the snowbanks at either side of the road, and sat there quietly. They sat and waited for the Germans to come along and kill them. Old men, young women with babies, children, all assembled quietly in the white expanse of their gravesites. The soldiers obliged methodically and efficiently. I may have wished to join those waiting to die if only to rest for a moment, for I didn't think my feet could still carry me. But Father held me firmly by the hand, as if sensing my temptation to join them. As the day wore on, increasing numbers of people left the long column, and soon the sides of the road were covered with crumpled bodies. The white snow hungrily devoured their red blood. In no time at all, the snow on both sides of the road no longer sparkled white in the bright sunshine, but in shades of red and pink. In the middle of the road the dark column wound on into the empty distance, while in back of it, discarded possessions littered the road like some new, strange species of snow flowers.

Mother, Sister, and Cousin Püppe walked as if mechanically propelled, but Father, strangely, seemed to recover some energy, warning us of grave dangers along this march. He seemed almost his former self as he instructed us to be neither at the head nor at the rear of the column where the Germans could take note of us easily. We were to shun the sides, lest others push us out of the column inadvertently and we would appear to be heading toward the snowbanks. Above all, he warned us not to fall or stumble, but to look down at all times, watching for icy patches. He murmured encouragement to each of us in turn, holding Mother's arm or my hand. One more step, he said, another and another, trying with only his words to give us strength.

While the column wound on through the still, white landscape, two hundred of us were separated from the rest and marched off on a side road to Sosnowice, a tiny village at the edge of a deep forest. We arrived as the sun was setting, having walked, run, and stumbled about eighteen miles from Parczew in less than ten hours. It was six days since we were driven from our homes, six days of cold, hunger, and thirst, six days of terror and murder. It took the eight hundred other Mielec Jews seven days to reach Włodawa—according to the telegram, they arrived on March 15, at half past six in the evening—so we two hundred could be considered lucky. The Germans chose Włodawa, Sosnowice, Radzyń, and Hrubieszów as destinations for the Mielec Jews because all were close to Sobibór, which by that time was nearly ready for its work of extermination, as was Bełżec with its three new gas chambers.

Major A. D. Ragger, in charge of the population and welfare section in Kraków, was pleased to report on March 13 that the Mielec *Aktion* would end three days later, on Monday, at exactly 1:12 p.m., when all Jews would have arrived at their destinations. He did not say—he didn't have to—that laggards, who might upset the predicted punctual arrival, would have to be killed. Hermann Höfle, who had handled the transports with admirable efficiency from his Lublin office in the appropriately named Schreckkaserne (barrack of dread), declared ever so truthfully on the afternoon of March 16, 1942, that Jews destined for Bełżec would never return to the General Government. And indeed, by autumn they had vanished from view, all traces of their existence erased. Much time passed before we learned who was dead and who survived. Long after the war's end, rumor still had it that someone was seen in such and such a place, or had been heard of by someone elsewhere; vain hopes were kept alive that relatives or acquaintances had somehow survived, and were alive and well in some far-off corner of the world. These were idle rumors, though, and soon even these last illusions were gone. After surviving the death marches, most of Mielec's Jews were murdered by the highly experienced Reserve Police Battalion 101 that was transferred to the Lublin district in July 1942.

FEBRUARY 1994

In October large mounds of persimmons suddenly appear in Jerusalem's markets and on greengrocers' stands. They are plump and soft and their color is unlike that of any other fruit. Persimmons began to be sold here more than fifteen years ago. They last throughout the winter, but by February, when Jerusalem, where I live, is enveloped in gray clouds, their price rises steeply, and sometime in March they are gone as suddenly as they appeared. I don't take the persimmons for granted. They may not be here again next year. I know all about people and things vanishing. Therefore, all winter long I eat the persimmons, thinking that for all I know these are the last persimmons I shall ever see.

The fleshy fruit has an unusual texture, and its appearance—a

reddish-orange-beige color, squat, neither quite round nor oval—
surprises me each time by its foreignness. Persimmons remind me
of nothing I knew when I was a child. We had red strawberries
then, reddish-pink watermelons, green and red apples, pale yellow
pears, dark blue blueberries—all with well-defined colors and
tastes, with none of the delicate ambiguities of persimmons.

Persimmons were not part of the landscape of my childhood,
the landscape that one thinks of as permanent and enduring
when one is a child. Even oranges, bananas, and pineapples were
considered great delicacies; the latter hardly ever seen, and tasted
perhaps once a year. But in Jerusalem these fruits are part of the
landscape, and when I walk up Aza Street and stop at Yomtov's
vegetable stand, staring in wonder at the profusion of colors and
shapes, I realize that the oddness is within me, that I am a stranger
here.

The old women in their baggy dresses and the brash young
mothers in their skintight pants who fill their plastic bags with
dark, purple grapes, shiny oranges, and delicate tangerines don't
doubt that Yomtov and his mounds of plump persimmons will be
here next October. Neither does Yomtov. Slightly cross-eyed, a
cap pulled low over his forehead, he stands behind the counter
and weighs and adds, adds and weighs. His four younger brothers
pack cartons of vegetables and fruit, and the delivery boy pedals
down Aza Street, unmindful of the heavy traffic. Yomtov, the
greengrocer, has been here for close to forty years. He has seen
young matrons grow into crotchety old ladies. He has seen penni-
less refugees become well-off. He has seen the neighborhood
change—newly rich young couples displacing the aging German
refugee population. He is a constant, standing behind the counter
all these years, weighing and adding. But I worry that, like a landscape of dreams, the persimmons together with Yomtov may vanish as if they had never been. My world is one of uncertainties; I

cannot take any part of it for granted. Like a traveler in strange parts, I am disoriented and the landmarks are unfamiliar.

Jerusalem is a city of stone. It stands on bedrock, and when a sewer or waterline needs repairing the workmen bring heavy machinery to drill through the rock of Jerusalem. Buildings are constructed of this stone, each stone patiently hammered and shaped by Arab workmen (as if in a reversal of Samuel's prophecy). Covered with white dust, the workmen sit surrounded by stones under a cloth canopy. Jerusalem was always a city of stone. All those who have ever been here—Israelites, Byzantine Christians, Crusaders, Turks, the British—have built houses of stone.

I walk down Mamilla toward Jaffa Gate. Some of its houses are already being demolished to make way for new, fashionable stone structures. The old houses are crumbling; some walls have tumbled down, exposing the neatly piled small stones between the thick outer and inner stone walls. The Mamilla houses date only from the Turkish Ottoman period. Yet soon the larger stones will be ground into smaller stones, and then into rubble and dust.

I go through Jaffa Gate and turn right toward the Armenian Quarter. I am surrounded by the old and yet ever-new life of smells and sounds of this strange city: sad-eyed donkeys with their heavy burdens; groups of tourists, their cameras ready to preserve the unaccustomed sights; Arab and Jewish shoppers heading down David Street toward the market where smells of freshly ground coffee and spices mingle with those of fragrant fruit and vegetables. I look at the silent remains of walls more than two thousand years old, stone neatly piled on stone, tightly fitting and still standing, though the walls' top stones fell down long ago, rolled away. The rubble and dust on which I walk today was once someone's house. I want to step gingerly on this dust because, since coming here, I understand the impermanence even of stones.

I brought to Jerusalem a picture of another Jerusalem not made of stone. It is a picture on a sukkah wall of my childhood in which Jerusalem is suspended between heaven and earth. House is stacked on house; the neat, tall stone houses creep up the mountainside and over the top. The painted Jerusalem had neither trees, nor streets, nor people. The mountain was surrounded by a wall. That picture of Jerusalem was not the Jerusalem of living, loving, joyful or sad people. No one I ever knew or ever heard of in Mielec lived in Jerusalem. To me it was the place where the Holy Temple once stood, where Solomon had judged, where pious people went to weep at the wall of the Temple that was no more. Jerusalem was not real the way other cities were, and therefore it did not strike me as odd that the sukkah picture showed no faces behind windows, or streets for people to walk in and children to play in, or trees for birds to sing in.

Jerusalem was in Zion. Zion was different from Jerusalem and Father had a song that began, "Zion, in the green fields, where the lambs pasture . . ." The Zion of my childhood was bright and sunny, the fields were only green, and the little lambs were white, woolly, and round. Next to those sunny green fields of my childhood Zion, Jerusalem was suspended between heaven and earth. I came to Jerusalem perhaps because of that picture, or perhaps because of Father's song, although it may have been neither of these. Perhaps I just thought a debt needed paying.

I taste the fleshy fruit of the persimmon. I watch ageless stones become new houses while others become the dust on which I walk. But I am a stranger here, because when walking in these sunlit, noisy streets, I also continue to walk through fields of snow and death where Father's song of Zion is no longer heard and where my childhood picture of Jerusalem was long ago torn to shreds.

CHAPTER TWO

═══════

MORE JOURNEYS

. . . she had ceased to believe in fathers [after] . . . they hurt her and he could not stop them. . . .

Thereafter she was no longer fully human, sister to all of us. Certain sympathies died, certain movements of the heart became no longer possible to her.

J. M. COETZEE, *Waiting for the Barbarians*

Sosnowice—a village of two rows of low, straw-covered huts on the road to Sobibór—was a tiny dot on the map. It was so poverty-stricken even potatoes were a luxury. The villagers called potato soup chocolate soup, perhaps because it was brown, or more likely because having never eaten chocolate they merely knew that it was very tasty. We were deposited in Sosnowice according to plan; there was to be no way of escaping from the village.

From a letter dated January 9, 1942:

Administrative District, Population and Welfare, Chełmno
Re: 2,000 Jews from Mielec

. . . I beg of you to make absolutely certain that at their final railroad stations the Jews are received and taken to the places you have selected for them. It must not happen, as has been the case, that Jews arrive unsupervised and then disperse throughout the countryside.

Indeed, dispersal was out of the question. As far as the eye could see there were only snow-covered fields and the forbidding forest. No other village or any kind of human habitation was in sight.

For nearly two months we lived in a flimsy hut owned by an old man, apparently a widower. The hut consisted of a kitchen and another room; the old man slept in the kitchen, the five of us in the room. Our hut was no worse than any of the others in the village. Built of boards with large cracks between them, it was almost as cold within as without. When the temperature dropped to forty or more degrees below zero, we were joined by the goat and chickens from the barn. Their rich animal smell mingled with that of unwashed human bodies, and their droppings called for caution when we moved about in the dark. Rats as big as kittens, but apparently starved into desperation, jumped all night to the low ceiling, trying to get at the food suspended from the rafters in pillowcases. Outhouses no longer existed; they had been dismantled long ago for patching or for firewood.

In spite of their poverty, or perhaps because of it, Sosnowice's Jews clung tenaciously to their religious practices, seemingly never questioning their fate. Each morning, the old man—a gentle soul in a brutal landscape with whom we shared this hut—rose before dawn. He poured water over his fingernails, wound the phylacteries around his head and arm, and began reciting the morning prayers. I would wake to the sound of his deep sighs and murmured blessings. He prayed long and ardently, apparently oblivious to the biting cold, while the goat dozed in the corner and the chickens pecked at invisible grain around his feet.

If the old man was put out over his uninvited guests, he did not say so. He rarely spoke to us, expressing neither displeasure nor sympathy. Even my badly frostbitten feet, now swollen out of all proportion, so that I could merely hobble about, did not move him to compassion; he neither inquired nor offered help. Having given us shelter in his only room, he treated us as part of his circumscribed existence. He did not question fate, or why things happened the way they did, why there were Germans, and why Jews were dropping in from unknown parts.

Not so the young girls, the old man's unmarried daughters perhaps, or other relatives—we never found out—who came regularly of an afternoon. They were robust, red-cheeked country girls, not a bit shy, who made themselves comfortable in our room and pulled out their knitting. They knew the most exquisite patterns and were pleased when we admired their handiwork. While the old man remained in the kitchen, praying or muttering to himself, we were sometimes ten or twelve in the little room, a crowd perhaps, but more easily keeping warm while the girls told their stories of life in Sosnowice.

Germans were not stationed in the village, though they did not forget the Jews, and appeared regularly to shave Jewish beards forcibly and administer beatings. Through the cracks of the hut's wall I watched the tortures they inflicted on the men, who silently endured pain and humiliation until they slumped to the ground. Apparently the Germans were much entertained by their work and the victims' passive endurance. They laughed boisterously as their sled disappeared down the road. Once they were gone, "our" old man would reappear in the kitchen from wherever he had been hiding.

Whether it was my painful feet, or utter exhaustion, or whether hunger and cold had sapped my energies, I remember becoming strangely quiet, indifferent to the happenings around me. Before the deportation from Mielec, I had asked questions, listened to everyone's discussions, worried about the family, about my friend Tośka. Now, in Sosnowice, I was barely aware that Uncle Reuven's family had not come with us. Vaguely I sensed that Tośka had disappeared forever. No one we had known in Mielec seemed to be in Sosnowice.

Passover came early in 1942, the first week in April. Not all the snow had melted, though the weather was now a little warmer. The old man had readied his tumbledown hut for Passover as if there were neither Germans nor dangers. He and one of his married daughters scrubbed and cleaned for an entire week before the festival and baked a dozen or so unleavened breads, the matzoh, which were shared like cake throughout the Passover week. Soap was not for sale here, and each family, preparatory to the cleaning, cooked its own soap using lye and lard. As the old man made his, he must have let his mind wander, for in the last stages, when the mixture foamed, the hot soap spilled over onto the range. It was a major catastrophe: The lard had rendered the stove ritually impure, and all cooking had to cease. To purify the range we had to gather enough wood to heat it to glowing red. Many days passed while we went hungry and were even more desperately cold than usual.

Meanwhile, both Mother and Father were fully occupied with finding flour for baking matzoh and other appropriate foods for the week-long holiday. Father was pleased with himself when he managed to have the baker bake him a pillowcase full, which he hung from the rafters. Thereafter and during the Passover week he had to get up each night to threaten the rats with extinction, even if they heeded him only while he stood over them. The moment he returned to bed they resumed their jumping, driven by hunger even greater than ours. Mother cooked several urns of beet borscht, which she lined up against the wall of our room. But by the time we started on our last urn, much to everyone's disgust it was discovered that a mouse had drowned in the soup. That year we did not have the ritual meal, the seder, because there was nothing to make a seder with—neither wine nor apples and nuts,

neither horseradish nor greens; none of the symbolic foods com-
memorating the exodus from Egypt were to be had in Sosnowice.
Indeed, how was it possible to celebrate deliverance from slavery
three thousand years ago when now we were apparently even
worse off than the Pharaoh's slaves? How could we say the hope-
ful words "Next year in Jerusalem," as one is supposed to, when
we barely dared hope to be alive in another year? We did not have
a seder in 1942, and four years would pass before I had a seder
again. That sederless though ritually observed Passover when
we were still together—Father's last Passover on earth when he
patiently protected our food from the rats, when Mother wept
over the spoiled borscht—has remained too painful a memory for
a truly joyful celebration ever since. Whatever made us into who
we were—Jews with a tradition, a past, a shared memory as much
the old man's as it was ours—was disappearing, was becoming
memory.

Uncle Reuven and his family, as well as the other Judenrat
families, had not been deported. They had arranged to go to
Radomyśl Wielki, having no doubt paid the Germans handsomely
for the opportunity. In 1942, a short reprieve could still be had for
money, as I learned many years later from another Radomyśl
escapee. I do not remember how Uncle Reuven contacted us in faraway Sosnowice, which did not have a post office, but one day,
some weeks after Passover, during spring's timid beginnings,
Korpantowa, the Polish family friend who had Mother's jewelry,
appeared. She was nervous, impatient, probably even frightened,
but she maintained nonetheless a commanding presence in this
desolate place. Tall and thin, her sparse gray hair severely pulled
back into a small bun, she towered over the village people, who
gathered around the horse-drawn cart in which she had arrived.
She had been sent by Uncle Reuven to take one of us away; it
didn't matter to her which one. There was no time, she urged, the

train would leave on schedule. It was decided to send me; I looked the least Jewish and spoke Polish fluently.

Without a backward glance, without regret, with a coldness of heart about the fate of my family that I am ashamed of to this day, I climbed on the wagon and drove off with Korpantowa to the railroad station in Parczew, the one we had arrived at two months earlier. I left Sosnowice without guilt or sorrow, aware that staying meant certain death. Although I don't remember Sobibór having been mentioned yet, Majdanek's notoriety had spread sufficiently for Mother to be convinced we would eventually end up in the concentration camp. Uncle Reuven probably paid well for the rescue, but then Korpantowa had been given Mother's jewelry. Although later that year she was no longer prepared to save a life, it is to Korpantowa's credit that she made the journey four more times, with considerable danger to herself, bringing the rest of the family to Radomyśl Wielki.

To this day, I can still see Sosnowice, this village at the edge of the dark, impenetrable forest where, it was rumored, partisans were hiding. I see the two rows of low, straw-covered huts strung out along the road that led through Sosnowice, and beyond the last house the flat, empty land. Except for the forest there were neither trees nor shrubs in this bleak landscape. Throughout the two months, I had looked at the forest with both longing and fear. I thought foolishly we might escape there, that the Germans would surely have no way of finding us in the dense woods. Perhaps the partisans would take us in, give us shelter and food, I fantasized, share with us their knowledge of the forest and how to survive in it. But I also feared the forest, the hungry wolves and wild animals that, I knew, lived in its deep shadows. To frighten me (it was never very hard), Cousin Esther had often talked about wolves, how they attacked human beings, especially children, dragging their bodies to the lair, slowly feasting on their entrails.

As it turned out, I did not venture into the forest around Sos-nowice, even after the snows had melted. In fact, I rarely ever left the hut. Outside, in the immense emptiness, I felt small and vulnerable, and the crowded hut where people came and went and young girls brought their knitting of an afternoon seemed a safe haven.

In summer the days were sunny and quiet in Radomyśl Wielki. It was a small town, not far from Mielec, though just how small I didn't know, because I never went far from the tiny room where the five of us had come to live. I had no interest in Radomyśl, the market, or who lived in the houses surrounding it, knowing that the town was merely another way station to another place. Cousin Esther and I sat on the doorstep in front of the house where our families each had a room, and we watched the people in the marketplace at their tasks: fetching water from the pump, buying a wedge of bread, bargaining with a peasant for an egg or butter. We no longer quarreled that summer as we had done in the past. We were sad and had little to say to one another. Sometimes I thought of Tośka, the friend I knew I would never see again, and I silently named the relatives—Mime Rivke and her daughters; Shime-Duvid, little Hayim-Yankel and his mother Hava—who had lived around the Small Market and who had vanished without a trace.

I thought of Mielec, so close by and yet so distant, as if in a different country. Home, our crowded room in Mielec, and the town's streets and markets already belonged to a long-ago past, to a different life whose outlines I by now only dimly recalled. Sometimes I tried to tell Esther about the hangar, the train, and Sos-nowice, but she only looked at me tiredly and nodded her head without responding. She did not rub her yellow teeth the way she had in the past, and when she spoke, which was seldom, her voice no longer had a sharp edge. Esther, it seemed, had become detached from everything around her. She had withdrawn into herself and had lost the need—or perhaps no longer cared—to inform me about the ways of this strange world. The adults no longer quarreled either. An unaccustomed peace had descended on the family, as if by common agreement we had decided to suspend our differences and animosities. I did not know then as I know now that we were waiting for the next deportation, which was about to occur.

Hans Frank, governor general of Poland, in a conference with the police, June 18, 1942:

> The Jewish problem demands a decision. Transportation facilities are needed, but for the next two weeks no trains will be available. Thereafter, increasing numbers of trains will have to be made available. The final liquidation of propertied Jews is mandatory.

Unlike the adults, I still had faith in Uncle Reuven. Hadn't he managed to save his family once before? Didn't he bring us back from Sosnowice? His connections with Germans, about which I knew nothing then, but which may have been known to Father and Mother, were still intact. Nearby, the Cyranka-Berdechow labor camp of Baeumer and Loesch, a road construction company in need of labor, was readied. Bizarre as it may seem today, the camp had been built by Jews, paid for with their own money. Malka, Cousin Esther's older sister, had been there since early summer. Uncle Reuven might have hoped to bring his family, perhaps even us, to the camp before the next deportation. But perhaps he no longer had enough money to pay for getting us into the camp. Or maybe everyone hoped that the Germans would overlook Radomyśl's existence, forget that it was there, forget the town's Jews. We waited. And while we waited, trapped in sleepy, sunny Radomyśl, I discovered the birds and their magic celebration of freedom.

Each morning, from the start of summer, I watched the birds in the tall trees around the marketplace. They began to sing and twitter as soon as the first light of the rising sun cast a purple glow over the far end of the square. I would open my eyes and, after climbing carefully over the sleeping bodies on the floor, tiptoe to the open window. At first the birds were invisible. I heard only the rustling leaves and the pure trills of some master singer. Then, when my eyes adjusted to the purple twilight, I could see one, two, five, dozens of birds, jumping from branch to branch, calling and answering one another.

Gradually the sky turned orange and the birds, obeying a secret signal known only to them, ventured out of the trees and gracefully spread their wings in a circle over the marketplace. Seemingly reassured of their ability to fly, a flock—hundreds, it seemed to me—rose into the orange sky to cruise in the early morning light. The birds flew wondrous patterns, close together and fanning out, separating and coming together, performing a magic airborne dance just for me, I felt, watching at the open window. Then, their morning exercise over, the birds settled on the rain gutters that ran along the roofs of the houses, chattering to each other while grooming themselves for the day ahead.

Meanwhile the orange had changed to pink and in the first bright rays of the sun the shadows faded from the doorways around the market below. The birds, no longer performers but audience, watched from their high perch as early risers opened and closed doors and went to draw water from the pump. The birds' delicate chatter became faint. Now there were other noises. Men and women cleared their throats, coughed, and spat; pails clanged; babies cried; pots banged; and in the distance peasants' wagons rumbled toward town. The marketplace was waking up, the magic performance had ended, and the birds dispersed. I would turn away from the window to face another day of waiting.

One morning in August things changed. I knew it the moment I awoke, for everyone was sleeping fully dressed, sheets knotted into bundles were scattered about the room, and Mother's checkered coat lay carefully folded at her side. Outside everything still seemed the same. The birds were beginning their morning song to the glowing sky; then the leaves rustled and the birds flew off. Slowly the shadows melted and the birds, their flight completed, came to rest on the gutters. But this day no doors were opened and closed. Pails didn't clang. The market remained as if asleep until suddenly the silence was shattered by the crude sound of motor-cycles and the terror-stricken cries of a great and still-invisible multitude. The deportation from Radomyśl Wielki and the sur-rounding villages had begun.

Its course was similar in broad outline to the deportation from Mielec, yet different. Again the Jews were collected in the market-place—those who were driven in like so many cattle from the out-lying areas and those who lived in the town. But instead of being marched away, the people were made to stand in a tightly packed mass to witness the house searches for hidden Jews, the "flushing out," as it was called.

We stood in the marketplace under the hot noon sun watching the horror unfold, as if invited to witness a macabre performance in which for a time at least we were spectators and not the per-formers. Loudly shrieking, crazed men covered with blood ran circles in the market until they fell and did not move again. Babies were flung from windows, landing with a thud on the gray cobblestones. Gunfire echoed through the narrow alleys behind the market as more and more people were found hiding. They ran here and there like frightened animals, thinking perhaps they could dodge the German bullets; their shrill screams reverberated in the alleys and market. Walls were smashed and doors broken down in search of hiding places. When finally these noises ceased, we, the masses in the marketplace, were once again assigned a part in the performance. We were made to stand in straight lines and then counted. Every tenth person was taken out and killed. Back in March on the icy road I had felt the nearness of death, the ease with which one can cease to be from one moment to the next. Now, on a bright summer day, under the lengthening shadows of the setting sun, death was again nearby, so terribly, arbitrarily close. The count went on, relentlessly and methodically, and those taken out to be killed did not leave a gap in the line, left no reminder that they had stood on a certain day on a certain spot in the Radomyśl market.

The day was nearing its end and we survivors were hurriedly marched out of town, once more on our way to an unknown destination. I did not avert my eyes from the slumped, sprawling dark shapes in the market, the scene of carnage, the red blood now dried an ugly brown on the gray cobblestones. A cooling evening breeze brought the sound of church bells from a distant village as we left the town behind us, their peaceful chimes mingling with the bursts of gunfire. Here and there cows still lingered in the pasture, but I had no eyes for them. What mattered again was staying in the crowd, not straying to the sides of the marching column where a bullet was sure to find its mark. What mattered was not to think of thirst or sore feet. Disconnected thoughts returned: Would the birds come back to the trees that night? Was Cousin Esther alive? Was this the end, or was there more to come? Would there be a tomorrow? For the moment, by mere chance, we had survived. We marched, stumbling on, interminably.

Finally we reached the Dębica ghetto. Here Jews of all backgrounds were collected from neighboring towns and villages and thrown together. For several days a familiar pattern repeated itself: Families were torn apart in ongoing selections, killings, and deportations. At night the trains rolled toward Auschwitz (no longer a secret to us), while those of us who were lucky enough to remain were among strangers. Our family of five was still intact, but we knew that it was the end of the road, that our luck had been stretched to the limit.

We were assigned a room in a hovel where the presence of the previous inhabitants, most likely already dead in Auschwitz, could still be sensed: dirty dishes from which they had eaten their last meal, a pot on the cold stove, some water in a bucket. I gave no thought to those who might have been here and were now gone. We were no longer squeamish.

We lived in Dębica less than three months in indescribable, vermin-infested squalor, in a leaky, windowless shack where energetic cockroaches scrambled for crumbs and rats roamed freely at night. The Dębica ghetto had been created from the poorest, most run-down section of town, with one of its sides, near our hovel, adjoining the marketplace. Uncle Reuven and his family lived in one of the few stone houses, several stories high. Now a member of the ghetto Judenrat, he was still an important man. But most of the people in the fenced-in area subsisted in shacks similar to ours. Hungry, sick, and destitute, sensing that the end was near in yet more selections and deportations to come, the people stole from one another and fought among themselves in an atmosphere of fear and suspicion.

Our family grew apart, as if we were creating distances among ourselves in preparation for the inevitable, as if each one of us in his or her own way turned inward to marshal the resources needed to somehow survive the next and final blow. Cousin Püppe worked outside the ghetto in a German office, assuring herself, she thought, a safe place when the next deportation came. She was convinced that "her Germans" would save her. The more she talked about it, however, the more the rest of us felt we were doomed. Sister had typhoid fever and in her weakened state hardly ever spoke. Mother had sunk into an apathetic stupor, capable of no more than caring for Sister in her illness and guarding her from being removed to the "hospital" where certain death awaited her. In the hospital the sick were no longer healed; periodically they were taken out to be shot to make room for new arrivals. Throughout Sister's illness, we constantly feared visits from Jewish policemen—victims turned into victimizers by the Germans—who might report her.

Only Father still seemed cheerful and concerned with our welfare while we retreated from one another and probably also from him. To be sure, he had stopped singing long ago, but he still smiled at me when he returned to the ghetto from the lumberyard where he carried boards on his shoulders from dawn till dusk. Each evening I waited for him near the ghetto gate; he had an uncanny ability to get bits of food—a shriveled apple, a crust of bread, a carrot—which he gave me and which I ate without even thinking of sharing them with either Mother or Sister. Ever since Sosnowice I had become greedy and selfish. At night, Father killed rats, doing so without obvious loathing. In fact, he killed rats almost gleefully, while I watched, hypnotized by the revolting spectacle, from my refuge on top of the table. He had found an axe and as soon as the rats arrived, which they did with suicidal regularity, he wielded his weapon, throwing the bloody remains across the fence in front of the Polish bakery. Gentle Father had turned fierce executioner, intent on the hopeless task of liquidating the Dębica rat population. We hated the bakery, for all day long we were tortured by its tantalizing smells of freshly baked bread. Throwing the dead rats at its front door was a small act of revenge for our misery.

I had launched into frenzied activity since arriving in Dębica. My major task was the daily trip to the soup kitchen where, being small and agile, I fought with the women for my place in the first row well before the doors opened. The soup kitchen was in a cellar and it was no mean feat to carry my pot of soup up the stairs, against the crowd that surged in the opposite direction. Watery and tasteless though the soup was, with only occasional pieces of potato or a morsel of cabbage floating in it, it seemed like a delicacy. Once a week I went to the ghetto bakery for our ration of bread. This could take the better part of a day and demanded great alertness both to keep my place in line and to detect short weight. The bakers were known to cheat, keeping some of the precious bread for themselves. The bread was dark, heavy, and moist, and I carried it home like a precious trophy. There was never enough of it. On market days I slipped through the ghetto fence, having found a loose board near our shack, to steal vegetables (we had no money to buy them) from the sharp-eyed peasant women. Hunger overcame fear; I cannot recall ever being afraid either of stealing or of being caught by the Germans.

When not busy obtaining food, I scrubbed the floor of our room and did laundry. I scrubbed the floor on my hands and knees to rid the rough wooden planks of the bloodstains from Father's rat slaughter, and I washed the clothes hoping to drown the lice and their eggs. Cleanliness became an obsession, as if being clean also meant living according to some kind of order, even though neither order nor cleanliness was possible. Laundry was a major operation. I had to collect wood for heating water and afterward, when the clothes were left to dry outside, I had to guard the few pieces from thieves as adept at stealing as I. Washing clothes, of course, did not rid them of the body lice firmly entrenched in seams and hems. Nor could we rid ourselves of head lice or the black fleas that feasted on us day and night. While we slept, fleas and lice were joined by armies of bedbugs. The search for nourishment went on relentlessly, both for us and for our vermin.

In those months, I probably came to resemble the half-starved ghetto children one sees nowadays in photographic exhibits. Ragged, with sharp features, but still quick-moving, I fought ruthlessly over anything that could be eaten. Occupied with my daily tasks, I forgot that I was still a child, and that once there had been a life of learning, books, friendships, and games. There was no time to waste on memories.

That autumn we did not observe the High Holidays. In Sosnowice, we did not celebrate the festival of spring; in Dębica, we no longer observed the holy days of autumn. They came and went with none of us paying attention, except Father perhaps. Maybe he even prayed, surreptitiously joining ten men for the prayer for the dead, the kaddish, for Grandmother Mindel. But there was neither a festive meal nor candle lighting. Observing holidays in the ghetto was forbidden. Father and Cousin Püppe went to work as they did every other day, seven days a week. The past with its celebrations of life, community, and history was no more.

Because I was so busy I saw Cousin Esther only rarely during those three months. She did not venture into the streets. Aunt Feige continued to manage their household affairs, and she apparently still had money to buy food, probably on the black market. Whenever I visited their room it smelled of cooking. Once, I even discovered a pot of food on a high shelf (too high for me to reach) in their toilet. Esther and I no longer had anything to say to each other. A gulf had opened between us, she on one side, seemingly succumbing to whatever was to be, I on the other, clinging with all my might to life with its crazy new logic, doing what I thought ought to be done by the living. Esther knew what was coming, I am sure, but as in Radomyśl she no longer cared to talk about it.

Uncle Reuven certainly knew. In the attic of their house, he secretly marked off a small space and built a brick wall, leaving a tiny opening through which we were to crawl when the day of the deportation came. He prepared a small heap of bricks, sand, and water for mortar, to fill in the opening after his family and mine were safely inside.

The evening before the start of the deportation, Mother suddenly collapsed. She was someone who seldom lost her composure, who was quiet and reserved. But now, faced again with calamity and death, she had come to the end of her resources. Her silence turned into loud, hysterical weeping. In the dim light of the oil lamp with its wick turned low so that deep shadows hid the corners of even this tiny room, Mother lay on the cot that had been Sister's sickbed and sobbed convulsively. While Sister sat by helplessly, never taking her eyes off the weeping figure, Father tried to comfort Mother, bringing her cups of water. I tried wiping her face with a damp rag. Nothing seemed to help. Finally, exhausted and still sobbing, she fell into uneasy sleep.

The familiar whirlwind of death and destruction began before dawn on a cold November morning. We ran to Uncle Reuven's hiding place through crazily surging and screaming crowds. It seemed as if all these people running through the narrow streets were looking for a last-minute escape, or perhaps they too had hiding places to which they were racing. Many came to ours, although it was supposed to have been a well-kept secret. Indeed, by the time we arrived, the small space was already filled to capacity and Uncle Reuven was frantically beginning to fit the prepared bricks into the opening. He himself was to remain outside, having apparently obtained the Germans' promise that as a member of the Judenrat he would be allowed to stay on in Dębica after the deportation, when the ghetto would be converted into a labor camp. I hoped Cousin Esther and Aunt Feige were in the attic, but

I did not see them immediately in the crush of old and young and babes in arms. Nor did I see Cousin Püppe. At first we thought she had been lost along the way, but some days later, the deportation having run its course and the train with the Dębica Jews having left for Auschwitz, we learned what happened to her. Someone who had jumped off the train brought us word that Püppe's Germans did not save her after all. Others urged her to jump from the train as they did, but she had become despondent and went to her death.

We were packed tightly into the confining space behind the brick wall, along with countless others. Breathing one another's breath, we were shoulder to shoulder and back to back; to move an arm or leg meant dislodging someone else's limb. To be in that attic with no possible escape should the Germans find us was a terrifying experience, as well as a supreme exercise in self-control. We were silent, as if afraid that someone was spying on us on the other side of the wall. The passage of time in the perpetual twilight was marked only by changing sounds that told us what was happening, for all of us up in that attic were by now seasoned deportation survivors. At first the ghetto was emptied of Jews. They were taken to a large pasture near the railroad tracks. We identified this stage by the people's shrieks and the German bellowing, punctuated by bursts of gunfire; people were always brutally beaten and killed during a deportation. When the noise died down, we knew that the selections had begun. Beatings and killings were now fewer. Later, we heard the arrival of the long train of freight cars. And still later, the mournful whistle of the locomotive told us that it was evening, and that the train was starting toward Auschwitz.

Once the train left, the familiar searches for hidden Jews began. The passage of time is not easily preserved in memory, and I cannot say just when the searches began, whether the day of the deportation or the one following. But we knew from previous experience that the Germans would search systematically, house by house, shack by shack, banging on walls, bursting into cellars, climbing up to attics. They knew very well how adept the Jews had become at hiding during deportations. This, of course, was the most dangerous time for us: We had to freeze, be absolutely still. We knew that for Jews found hiding there would be certain death. Despite our having approached the limits of endurance, now was the real test; only now, during the search, was life or death to be decided. A cough, a sneeze, a moan, the slightest noise, could reveal the hiding place.

The search may have lasted minutes, half an hour, or more; when death is that close, all thinking ceases and time is not remembered. What remains in memory is the indescribable fear, and vague images and sounds. We heard the Germans' harsh voices on the other side of the wall; we heard the snorting of their vicious dogs. We did not breathe or move. Finally, we heard their heavy footsteps going down the stairs. Through the grimy attic window we watched them leave the house. Death had been as close as one flimsy brick wall. As the Germans were leaving, a baby died, suffocated by her own mother. A man went berserk and had to be tied up and gagged. I watched without emotion, memorizing, not knowing that I would live to write these words, inadequate to describe what I had witnessed.

We thought we were saved. Such are the delusions of human beings for whom, when confronted with death, only the moment counts and not the moment after. Surviving the deportation was not enough, though as far as the machine of destruction was concerned we no longer existed. We were on the train to Auschwitz, or already ashes. How to remain alive and what to do next were the crucial questions. There was a list of those who could remain in Dębica and only Uncle Reuven and Mother were on it. I am sure he was responsible for Mother's name being on the list. She was a typist and Germans were very fond of neatly typed reports, letters, and various other communications. He had taken advantage of that. But at the same time, he had been unable to save his own wife and daughter, or the rest of us.

SEPTEMBER 1980

The ride from Kraków, where I am staying on this journey to Poland, to Dębica leads through pleasant fields, distant small woods, and picturesque villages. Here and there some old thatched-roof houses remain, with tall sunflower stalks behind neat picket fences. The driver, a talkative man, tells me he was born the day before Germany's capitulation. Everywhere, he says, pointing to the right and left of the road, Jews lived in villages and towns before the war. They went away, says the driver, and now not a single Jew remains. He does not lie, nor does he wish to deceive; after all, he has never seen a Jew (as far as he knows), and has no reason to doubt what he has been told by his elders and teachers. In normal times it is not assumed that people who go away are being driven away, to be killed.

The driver was puzzled when I asked him to take me to Dębica. On our previous drive to Mielec in his comfortable touring car he had invented a history for me: I was the daughter of a Polish mother who had taken me, as a child, to America. Although never having seen my homeland, he reasoned, I had learned Polish and now at last had come to see Mielec, the ancestral home, for the first time. Why would I want to see Dębica? he asked. Did I have family in Dębica? I'm sure it didn't occur to him that I might be Jewish, and I, for my part, felt somehow at ease with the identity bestowed on me. Old terrors were kept in check, old ghosts safely banished. Later I would be amused by the ease with which I reverted to the role of a Polish girl that on a previous journey had saved my life.

We arrive in Dębica by midafternoon and ask directions to the marketplace. Younger people shake their heads; there is no marketplace here, they say. At last an old-timer shows us the way to a park with tall trees, saying that this is where the market was before the war. To locate the area where the ghetto had been—our family's last stop before we each went on to live or die—will not be easy, I realize. But finding the place, pointing to the spot where it all ended, has become all-important.

I leave the driver in the park that had once been the marketplace and tell him I want to take a walk. He sits down contentedly on a park bench between two pipe-smoking old men. The place is crowded. Girls stroll arm in arm, couples flirt, tough-looking young men in unfashionably cut trousers lean against lampposts. No one here seems plagued by unerasable memories. Older women with shopping bags bustle through the park to stand in one line or another to buy food, as Poles seem to be doing everywhere. A vendor wheels a little wagon with lemons into the park and a line immediately forms; the limit is one lemon per customer.

The day is overcast, enveloping houses and even green trees with a kind of gray tinge that I will always associate with this part of Poland. It is a cheerless, chilling gray day, although it is not quite autumn. I leave the park, determined to find at least the outlines of the ghetto. Something should be there, some reminder of its existence.

I am on a pleasant, tree-lined street with houses on one side newer than on the other. The new houses are large, uniform blocks—probably workers' apartments, and, no doubt, built after the war. Across the street are smaller and older single-family dwellings in fairly good repair, interspersed with other residential buildings several stories high. A long line has formed outside one of the shops ahead of me, and as I approach I smell the unmistakable aroma of freshly baked bread. All at once it is clear: The street on which I stand had been the dividing line between the Polish section and the ghetto, with the fence running down the middle. Today's large housing blocks in back of me must have been built on the rubble of the ghetto area that was torn down after the final deportation, or after the end of the war to make room for the new housing.

Indeed, I am certain that directly across the street from the bakery is more or less the spot where our rat-infested shack must have been. I wonder whether any of the elderly people in the park still remember the ghetto and its suffering humanity. Probably not. For some, forgetting is easy. Together with the houses and hovels, memory too was, no doubt, obliterated. The realization hardly comforts me, nor does having found this portion of the ghetto. I had thought that, pointing to the spot, I could say: Here, here is where we suffered, here it all finally ended. Naming the place, I thought, would help me find whatever it was I lost. It didn't.

My mother, father, sister, and I sat on the floor of the dark house we had found after leaving the attic. There were only the four of us now. Around us lay sleeping bodies, helter-skelter, as if they had dropped off to sleep wherever they happened to be. They were strangers we had never seen before who had crawled out of their hiding places—hungry, thirsty, without even enough spittle to wet their lips—just as we did when the searches ended. They, like us, had sought refuge in this empty, broken-down house within the ghetto that after the deportation had become a labor camp. They, like us, hoped that for another day, two more days, the house would be part of the camp and not outside of it.

I was too tired and hungry to worry much about where Cousin Esther and her mother were. I had lost sight of them after we

finally stumbled, one by one, out of the attic. My only vivid memory was of the woman who carried the child she had smothered
during the search. She carried the small body, like a sacrificial
offering, down the staircase and handed it to her waiting husband
in the street.

Father sat hunched over next to Mother. They did not speak.
He shifted uncomfortably, his posture one of dejection and hope-
lessness. For the first time since the deportation from Mielec he
seemed to have come to the end of his resources. I felt, without his
saying so, that he no longer knew what to do, what plans to make,
how to save his family from destruction. For nine months he had
taught us how to survive and how to remain alive. He never once
gave up, even if with each deportation, with each journey, our
chances of survival decreased. He always supported, helped, tried
to make us believe that somehow we would make it, defy death one
more time. Now, seeing no way out, he had become hopeless and
helpless. At last he had to confront the breakup of the family—
only Mother and Uncle Reuven could remain in what was now the
Dębica labor camp.

I realized then that Father had to leave Mother if he was to save
himself. Sister and I would have to leave as well. But Father was
still not prepared to face the end of the family. Only many years
later, when I had children of my own, would I try to understand
(without really being able to) Father's terrible struggle between his
love for us and his fear for our lives, his desire to protect us and his
stubborn denial that he was unable to do so. He understood and
yet did not that he no longer played a part in our ultimate fate.
Father was losing the essence that gave meaning to his existence.
He could not accept losing us. But in Dębica I ceased to listen to
Father's voice. I heard only my own, which clamored for life. My
mind was made up: I would leave and I would leave alone. On my
own I had a chance, I felt; someone might hide me. On my own I

would find a way. Didn't Korpantowa have Mother's jewelry? If not Korpantowa, someone else would take pity on me. In my heart I had already abandoned Father and Sister to their fate, feeling once again, as in Sosnowice, neither remorse nor guilt. I had made my choice.

We sat on the floor of the dark house, Father, Mother, Sister, and I, each isolated from the others by a wall of unsharable fear and hunger. The penetrating cold of the room seemed to have chilled our very souls.

As if exhausted by his struggle, Father was resting on a broken bed in the corner of the room. The bedding had been slit open and most of the feathers had spilled out, clinging to our shoes and clothing and getting into our hair. He shivered under the ruined bedding. There were fewer people in the room than during the previous night. Perhaps they had found other houses to hide in. Or perhaps they had escaped to the forest. Someone had brought a candle. Its weak flicker cast eerie shadows on the walls, grotesquely elongating the ragged, silent shapes of the fugitives.

I sat next to Father and held his hand. I looked into his drawn face that no longer offered any comfort. His eyes were closed, but he did not sleep. I wanted to talk to him. I wanted to tell him that I must leave, that I didn't want to be shot, that I didn't want to die. I wanted to live, and I wanted his permission to go away. I wanted his approval. I don't know what I finally said, but I will never forget his answer: Don't go, he said, don't leave the family. We must stay together, he said. Don't go. Those were his last words to me.

I must have spoken to Mother, though I don't remember telling her of my plan to go to Mielec and find someone to hide me. Unlike Father, she accepted my decision, and I knew she would help me escape. Before dawn she and I quietly slipped out of the room. Father spoke to neither of us—had Mother told him? He sat on the broken-down bed, his shoulders hunched over and his head sunk low on his chest. He did not look at me when I pulled the door shut.

There was no moon. The air was misty, blurring the outlines of the crude, empty shacks where no one lived any longer. Staying close to the walls of the huts, we made our way to the edge of the camp. My mother must have chosen this spot with great care—it was not near the market where we had lived, and where a solitary figure walking across would have easily been seen. Instead she guided me to another part of the newly created camp, adjoining a dark street with houses on the opposite side. There a temporarily strung barbed-wire fence separated Jews from gentiles. She must have reasoned that in this spot I could easily melt into the dark shadows of trees and houses. When we reached the last shack, Mother pushed some money into my cold hands, enough for the train fare to Mielec, she said. I don't know who had given her the money. Was it Uncle Reuven's last gift to her, or to me? She hurriedly whispered for me to dig under the barbed wire, but to watch for the searchlight and to stay low to the ground. Take the train to Mielec, said Mother. Go to Korpantowa and ask her to hide you. She has our money and my jewelry. Mother kissed me briefly and ran her hand over my cold face as if trying to imprint its contours on her hand. As if in response to my urge to live, she had found an awesome strength born of total despair—was she sending me to live, or to certain death? Quickly crawling toward the barbed wire, I didn't look back, but I knew she would be watching and listening long after I had disappeared.

Now I was totally alone, dependent only on myself. I frantically dug the wet soil under the barbed wire with my bare hands, crouching low when the searchlight swept over me. There was no time to think about fear, or what might happen next. I dug. I crawled. I made it to the other side, down a short incline, and then to the road.

But I see, as I read over these sentences, that I have made it sound too easy, too simple. Fears may not have entered my thoughts then, but fears were in my belly, cramping my bowels. Can anyone really know what the fear of death is like if he has never experienced it? Can sickening, poisonous fears be described at all?

After reaching the road and on my way to the railroad station, I had to be especially careful and keep my wits about me. Now I had to concentrate on becoming someone else, and assume the role of a Polish girl who showed none of the fears of the Jew. I imagined being sent off by my Polish parents to visit an ailing grandmother, to help out in the house. I had blonde hair. My features did not match those considered typically Jewish—something I was aware of since my forays in the Dębica market. But I needed to guard my eyes; Germans, it was said, recognized Jews by the look in their eyes. As I approached the ticket window another fear took over. Would my brown eyes, which should have been blue were I really Polish, give me away? Would my dirty hands arouse suspicion? Yet, pretending came easily—later in life it would become a familiar game.

Only the barest outline of that long day when I walked the crossroads of life and death remains in my memory. First there was the train ride to nearby Mielec with its short reprieve from fear in the train's dark shadows. Then came the onset of new fear: What if someone recognized me in Mielec, or denounced me to the Gestapo, or to Rudi Zimmermann? Would I be taken to the Gestapo house and tortured? What if I did not find my way to Korpantowa? After all, I had never gone to her house by myself, being considered too young to go such a distance alone. The train ride ended all too soon.

By the time I arrived in Mielec, a snowstorm had covered houses and fields in uniform white. Familiar landmarks were obliterated and I was soon lost in the snow-covered fields. The road to Korpantowa's house had disappeared under a blanket of soft, white snow. Finally, I found my way there. My resolve to live soon wavered though when Korpantowa, cursing viciously, untied her snarling black dog to chase me away. For a time I thought that I must surely die in the bitter cold, and I remembered stories about people who fell asleep in the snow never to wake again. I don't think I felt anger toward Korpantowa then. At such a time one cannot afford to waste precious strength on either anger or self-pity.

Somehow I kept going that long, cold day, though I cannot remember how. I went on in spite of snow and my wet, heavy shoes, in spite of fatigue and hunger. I returned to town and sought out the landlord of the house where we had lived. I recall this encounter most vividly. He was drunk, and neither his bony wife nor their small twin girls who always clung to him were at home. He sat alone at the table, a bottle of vodka in front of him, and he looked at me with bloodshot eyes, perhaps in recognition or perhaps not. Although he was not a large and powerful man like Korpantowa's husband, he terrified me by the way he touched me and pulled me toward him. I did not know then what men were capable of doing, but I sensed the danger and knew that I must get away from him at once. Terror-stricken, I fled from the house, leaving behind me a large puddle of melted snow into which the drunken landlord stared with incomprehension.

Terror was followed by despair—draining, bottomless despair. Darkness had fallen and the world was becoming ever less recognizable. Every shadow was grotesquely misshapen and spelled new danger. There were streets I seemed never to have seen before, unfamiliar houses. I knew mothers were in warm kitchens cooking supper; bright oil lamps were on their tables, children were doing homework— they were inside, and I was outside in the bitter cold. I no longer had the strength to be afraid, though I was sure I would die in the white, cold snow, forgotten, alone, abandoned.

The snow had let up but the streets were freezing over rapidly in the bitter cold of the night. Stumbling through unfamiliar streets, often unable to keep upright on the slippery ice, I came at last by some strange miracle to the Orlowskys' apartment. Was it a prayer that guided me? More likely, I had asked a rare passerby in the street if he or she knew where the Orlowskys lived. I might even have asked more than one person, until someone pointed the way. To this day I don't know how it occurred to me to seek the Orlowskys out as a last resort. But except for Korpantowa and the landlord, I did not know any other Polish gentiles in Mielec. Mother had not mentioned the Orlowskys, assuming apparently that Korpantowa would take me in.

The Orlowskys were devout Catholics and Polish patriots from Poznań. Shortly after the German invasion of Poland, they had declined becoming German citizens, and had come to Mielec as refugees. They had rented the cellar apartment in the building in which we had lived. As neighbors and, in a manner of speaking, fellow sufferers, we had exchanged courtesies, but never more than that. We lost contact with them after they moved. Leokadia Orlowsky was a delicate woman, suffering from a heart condition; her husband, Stanisław, a tax clerk, drank too much, as did many Polish men. I did not play with their daughter, Roma, while they lived in the cellar. She was younger than I and she went to school, whereas Jewish children were forbidden to attend school.

I came to their apartment after dark, drenched and nearly frozen. Even if I don't know how I got there, I remember standing dazed in the kitchen doorway, suddenly feeling the rush of warmth, inhaling the perfume of long-forgotten home smells, seeing the golden glow of the brightly burning oil lamp on the table under the window. An eternity, it seemed, had passed since I had seen a home. There were two beds piled high with featherbedding against the wall, a large ceramic tile oven opposite, a table and chairs. Mrs. Orlowsky pulled me inside, bolting the door and making sure the curtains were drawn. Has anyone seen you? she asked. Then she gave me dry clothes, warmed my frozen feet, fed me, and later hid me in the chicken coop. Eventually, perhaps after some days had passed, she told her husband. Confronted with the facts, he did not have the heart to send me away, though he may have wanted to. The journeys had ended for a time.

SEPTEMBER 1997

Historians have forgotten Dębica, and Radomyśl Wielki. After all, historians cannot be expected to remember every small ghetto and every minor deportation where only a few thousand Jews (was it eight thousand, as many as ten thousand?) went to their death and where only a few hundred were gunned down or clubbed to death. The historian must concern himself with the larger questions, which presumably distance from the past allows him to do. He has to account for six million—how can he possibly pay much attention, if any, to that small dot on the map, Dębica, where one cold and gray autumn day only thousands were taken to die. I could fault historians for their omissions, their neglect, or their forgetfulness. Yet I too forget even as I remember. The images that pass before my eyes as I write are sometimes painfully vivid, at other times vague, mere shadows. I am unable to decipher them and the portions of the past to which they belong.

Forgetting comes more easily in New York, Chicago, or Boston than in Jerusalem. But even here remembering is harder lately, as crumbling stone walls are crushed by merciless bulldozers and old houses in neglected gardens make way for fashionable high-rises. I walk up Herzl Boulevard toward Yad Vashem, the Holocaust

Memorial. On my right is the military cemetery with its countless graves of young men who fell in wars that some now say may have been unnecessary. Ahead is the red Alexander Calder sculpture, which juxtaposes ephemeral modernity and the timelessness of concrete death. A short walk to the right of the Calder brings me to Yad Vashem. Buses unload hundreds of tourists with their video cameras; busloads of soldiers on a day's outing mill cheerfully about the kiosk; noisy schoolchildren with their teachers arrive; delegations of businessmen with their own guides alight from minibuses—there is a kind of carnival atmosphere in the bright Jerusalem sunshine. Soon all will fall silent during the visitors' twenty-minute guided tour of the museum and its pictures of death and destruction.

I leave tourists and soldiers behind and walk down to the Valley of the Communities, past wooded hillsides, past the cattle car absurdly perched over a precipice, past the memorial tablets to righteous gentiles. Down there, on the very bottom of the wadi, is the Valley of the Communities, to which tourists don't always come. Stone is piled on stone there, huge blocks of golden Jerusalem stone, with inscribed names of thousands of cities, towns, and villages where Jews once lived and prospered, and then were no more. The names of communities in France, Belgium, Germany, Russia, Czechoslovakia, and elsewhere are inscribed in larger and smaller letters, high up so that I have to crane my neck to see, or low down near the ground. Here are neither trees nor shrubs, nor is the song of birds heard. There is only the deep silence of dead stone. But here are the stories of Mielec, Wieliczka, Dąbrowica, Dębica, and Radomyśl, and I take heart. Even if mortal historians will not remember these stories, because they are engraved in durable stone it may take a little longer to forget them—perhaps until the day when no one is left to listen to the stories the stones tell.

CHAPTER THREE

WHEN GRANDMOTHER DIED

Everyone who remembers a war first-hand knows that its images remain in the memory with special vividness. The very enormity of the proceedings, their absurd remove from the usages of the normal world, will guarantee that a structure . . . for ready narrative recall will attach to them.

PAUL FUSSELL, *The Great War and Modern Memory*

There was a time before the journeys began. It was child-hood, a time of books and learning, games and friendship, of love and trust, of quarrels, serious while they lasted, soon forgotten when they were over. It was a time when as far as I was concerned everyone I knew was exactly in the place where they belonged and were the way they should be. It was a time that for many years thereafter I thought had been a dream, until I went to Mielec and found houses, streets, and markets precisely where in my mind's vision I had placed them.

As a child I saw a pervasive order in the way we lived. It was not an ideal order, by any means, for there was much that was unpleasant, or ugly, and much that I disliked. But life had an orderliness and a rhythm. The rhythm centered around holidays with their special customs and foods, and the weekly Sabbath— Friday afternoons I took the large cholent pot (which contained our Sabbath meal, a concoction of potatoes, onions, beans, and meat) to the bakery for cooking overnight in the hot brick oven. At my age, this order was comforting, though I am sure today that to my older sister and others her age it may have been suffocating, as eventually it might have become for me had I grown older in Mielec. I often ask myself who I might have been then, what kind of person I might have become, had a way of life and a way of being not vanished so completely and suddenly, leaving behind only a memory of death and destruction.

Grandmother Mindel, my father's mother, was the central figure in our lives. Even he deferred to her. At the turn of the century her husband, Hayim-the-Large, had built a two-story stone house on Sandomierska Street, a store on the ground floor and a three-room apartment above. I think he died soon thereafter, and I never found out why he was called Hayim-the-Large. Most likely it was to distinguish his side of the family on the major market, the Large Market, from Hayim-the-Small and his branch of the family around the Small Market. Most memorable about Grandmother were her large nose and the yellow everyday wig that she changed for a gray one on the Sabbath. Broad-hipped, wearing several skirts one on top of the other, she stood behind the counter of her store guarding the money drawer. Behind the other side of the L-shaped counter stood Uncle Reuven (whom people called Rivele), who always stared dreamily at some distant point high up on the wall, until sharply told by Grandmother to fetch pickles from the barrel for a customer, or to bring her the sugar someone else wanted, or to do some other chore. He was a thin man with a thin mustache who had married into our noisy, squabbling Geminder family. As the outsider, he carried no weight in the family; perhaps he joined the Judenrat after the Germans came in order finally to assert himself.

Aunt Feige, his wife, was as different as could be from quiet, self-effacing Uncle Reuven. Short and broad-hipped like Grandmother, she was in perpetual motion—running up the wooden staircase to the apartment, down to the store, to the marketplace, to a neighbor, back to the store to wait on customers or to order her husband to fetch and carry.

While Grandmother Mindel's Jewish customers up and down Sandomierska Street bought by the gram, or at most a half-kilo, Polish customers like Korpantowa purchased whole sacks of flour, dried beans, and peas. Whenever Korpantowa came, Uncle Reuven was required to load the sacks onto her horse-drawn droshky. As a friend of the family and a valued customer Korpantowa received special treatment—Aunt Feige would get for her from the market women an oval white cheese, or butter wrapped in green leaves. Grandmother's German customers from Czermin were treated well too. The Zimmermanns with their dour son Rudi drove up in a horse-drawn wagon from their village, and Uncle Reuven, under Aunt Feige's watchful eyes, carried sacks of flour and fetched and carried sugar and lentils.

After these large purchases, Grandmother and Aunt Feige would often start arguing. Grandmother might decide she had been shortchanged (she was rather tightfisted), or Feige might accuse her of hiding money. Whatever the reason, the two women fought fiercely, while Uncle Reuven quietly slipped out of the store and was gone. I quite enjoyed the shouting and commotion because to me this was a part of, and not a departure from, order. Most people up and down Sandomierska Street quarreled at one time or another with their relations.

Cousin Esther and I quarreled a great deal too, especially when she, only two years older than I, taunted me with her knowing things I did not. I did not really like Cousin Esther with her stringy brown hair and her large yellow teeth, which she was in the habit of slowly rubbing back and forth. She may not have liked me much either, but each of us was often all the company the other one had, so we played dominoes, or played with paper dolls, especially if her older sister, Malka, could be cajoled into drawing fashionable dresses for them. We often argued and then were *brogis*—the Yiddish term for not being on speaking terms with another person. Reconciliation took place in accordance with a ritualized order. We found intermediaries who conducted the negotiations with us over the concessions each of us was willing to make. As for Grandmother and Aunt Feige, I don't know by what means they settled their arguments; but after each shouting match they returned to managing the store as if nothing had happened.

The older girls seemingly never argued with their friends. Cousin Malka, her long braids tucked behind her ears, sat upstairs joking and laughing with her girlfriends while doing needlework. My sister was apprenticed to a dressmaker, though dressmaking was a job she hated. But she never argued with Mother over it. Nor did I ever hear arguments between her and Cousin Püppe. The two girls got along famously and, when not at work, visited with Cousin Malka. And Mother never quarreled with anyone, even when my father was angry with her. Her equanimity, reassuring to me, must have been supremely annoying to others. Therefore, as I saw it, some people did and some didn't get along, and whether they did or didn't was part of a perfectly natural order.

The summer months in 1939 were unusually bright and sunny. Mother would send Cousin Esther and me to drink fresh goat's milk at a farm, convinced that it was better for us than boiled cow's milk. We walked through the golden wheat fields, picking bright blue cornflowers and red poppies that grew in profusion along the way. In spite of its presumed therapeutic qualities, the goat's milk did little for Cousin Esther, who remained as puny and pale as ever, and she still rubbed her yellow teeth. In summer Grandmother Mindel switched from cooking chicken soup to plum soup, which I liked much better and which we ate in the "good" room upstairs. Sabbath afternoons, Uncle Reuven, Father, and their friends sat in the kitchen (it doubled as Grandmother's bedroom), drinking beer and eating salted chickpeas, while the women gossiped in Aunt Feige's bedroom. The older cousins paraded demurely up and down Kolejowa Street, which they called Broadway—invariably an American city's most fashionable street, they thought.

That summer I saw my first Yiddish drama. Throughout the spring, some of the young people, members of a small group of amateur actors in Mielec, had been rehearsing a musical they selected from Father's collection of librettos, kept in a box in the attic. Its theme, beloved by Yiddish-speaking audiences, was that of a young man betrothed to the most beautiful girl in town, to whom he swears eternal love before leaving for America. She waits faithfully for years on end until at last he returns, rich and famous, having meanwhile completely forgotten her. I don't remember what happened to the heroine, but I know it was sad. Perhaps she became an old maid, a fate considered terrible at the time. The melodrama was stupendously moving and to this day I can still sing one or two of its arias. I had seen the rehearsals but was not permitted to attend the performance, which was meant only for adults. Nonetheless, while the audience went wild, I watched from under a bench in the auditorium and wept bitter tears when Naftule Birnbaum, the baker's son, sang the role of the faithless lover.

That summer I too had one glory-filled moment onstage when the Beit Ya'akov, the religious school for girls that I attended, gave its end-of-the-year performance. With a black eyebrow pencil, Sister had lovingly transformed me into a chimney sweep. I wore a tall hat and I played a song on my recorder. Father was inordinately proud of me and I decided then and there that I was destined for a career in the theater.

But that summer there were also rumors of trouble brewing, of German armed might, of war. The older cousins, Püppe and Aunt Sheindl's two daughters, sang a satiric song about British prime minister Neville Chamberlain to the tune of a popular song—no one was fooled by Chamberlain's efforts at appeasement, except the man himself, I suppose. Apparently there was some talk about sending us young ones out of harm's way, but Grandmother decreed that the family must not be split up. So in spite of danger signals the adults were receiving, we all remained where we were, in Mielec, under blue skies and surrounded by fields of golden ripening wheat.

And that summer Grandmother Mindel died. She died early one Saturday morning in August. Hava, from Father's side of the family, and little Hayim-Yankel, her son, brought us the news when we were still in bed. Father was not at home. Apparently he had stayed with Grandmother during her final hours. His sister, Sheindl, and her family lived in the room adjoining ours, and the moment Hava arrived the whole family broke into loud wailing. Mother, who was never easily ruffled, took Hava into our room and seated her next to the little brass table. Hava lifted Hayim-Yankel onto her lap and sobbed uncontrollably, repeating over and over what a saintly woman, a soul without peer, my grandmother had been.

Hava was part of the sprawling clan of interrelated families of Hayim-the-Small from around the Small Market. She had no husband, she may not even have been married; such matters were never spoken of in front of children. Together with the five- or six-year-old Hayim-Yankel (which people pronounced "Ham-Yankel"), she seemed to spend all her time visiting one or another of the relatives. She was an emotional woman, small and quick-moving, with wild gray hair and piercing black eyes. Winter or summer, she wore a long dark skirt and a large colorful shawl. Hayim-Yankel was invariably dressed in a sailor suit. He was a pale child with a constantly stuffy nose who whined a great deal. Hava paid little attention to his complaints, except to force bites of food into his mouth. No one called Hava crazy, as they often did the woman who lived on the corner of the Small Market and, staring vacantly, went about muttering to herself. Yet there was something odd about Hava, something not quite right, and some people said she had the evil eye.

Mother was not superstitious. She believed in neither evil eyes nor the ways to avert them, and that Saturday morning she talked quietly and gently to Hava, trying to comfort her. I crawled back under the feather cover, not knowing what to do. I would have liked to cry the way Hava and my aunt and cousins were doing in the next room, and I felt guilty because no tears came no matter how hard I tried. I had a hard time mourning for Grandmother Mindel because I knew she had never been fond of me, nor I of her. Grandmother cared for only two people in her family: her only son, my father, and Cousin Esther. She bought sweet oranges for Esther and gave her pieces of chocolate when she thought I wasn't looking. So that Saturday morning all I could do was think of Grandmother, how she looked, walked, and talked, and how it seemed she had stopped doing so now. But even though I knew that somehow someone dead meant a person being no more, I could not conceive of Grandmother no longer standing in the store behind the counter, arguing with Aunt Feige, or lying in her huge bed in the kitchen with the kerchief tied around her shaven head.

Only a few days earlier she had had one of her fierce quarrels with Aunt Feige. Grandmother had decided to close the store during the busiest hours of the day, pulling the heavy iron shutters closed, locking them with her enormous key, and hiding the key in her bed. Shouting and cursing, Aunt Feige ran upstairs and tore Grandmother's bed apart, tossing skirts, wigs, bits of crackers, shoes, underwear, and pillows out of the bed until she found the key. Grandmother knew a curse or two herself and shouted them while pulling on Feige's arms, trying at the same time to collect her belongings, which flew in all directions. Finally, brandishing the key, Aunt Feige triumphantly retreated down the stairs to reopen the store, with my grandmother in hot pursuit. The two of them still shouting, one tried to turn the key while the other tried to pull it out of the lock. Uncle Reuven was nowhere to be seen and eventually passersby made peace between mother and daughter. It was odd to me that Grandmother, so vigorous only a few days ago, was now silent, gone, never to be seen again.

I knew little then about death and dying. Occasionally there were dead animals, a mouse in the mousetrap, but dead mice were different from people dying and disappearing. In Mielec there were two cemeteries, one old and one new. Great-grandfather Israel, a peddler, who had made the rounds of villages with his backpack delivering goods the peasants had ordered, was buried in the old cemetery, as was his son Hayim, Grandmother Mindel's husband. I didn't know where this old, and by now full, cemetery was. The new cemetery was at the end of Kolejowa Street, near the railroad station, but I had never been inside the low-walled enclosure. Cemeteries were among the places to be avoided, we children believed. Certainly, the dead, I thought then, did not disappear entirely after they were buried. Something of who and what they were must remain in the cemetery. How else would they be able to follow the Messiah (in whose eventual appearance we children absolutely believed) to the Holy Land when he came? And what, after all, was the purpose of the little bag of soil from the Holy Land that people were buried with, if not to help guide the dead to their destination?

I remember once questioning Father about the Messiah's coming. Being close to the railroad station, I suggested, enabled the dead to catch the train to the Holy Land when the Messiah came.

They wouldn't have to walk far—a good thing, considering that old people (since only the old died) walked with difficulty. The Messiah too had to be doing a great deal of walking about to collect the dead. With the railroad close by, he could save time. Father seemed rather embarrassed by these speculations. Still, he did not try to dissuade me from my messianic expectations; neither did he explain death and dying. I came to doubt the Messiah's coming on my own not long thereafter.

Grandmother's death led to much turmoil, and it was decided to send Cousin Esther and me to Korpantowa during the seven days of mourning. Korpantowa lived some distance from town in her pleasant house surrounded by a white picket fence and guarded by her vicious black dog, who would terrorize me when three years later I returned to Mielec. She and her husband had no children and he probably did not like or approve of his wife's Jewish friends. Korpantowa's husband had an enormous stomach over which bobbed his pink, clean-shaven head, reminding me of a balloon of the kind Mother bought for me when the circus came to town. One might have thought him jolly, but he was not. He never smiled and rarely spoke, and I never saw him in Grandmother's store.

Korpantowa did not like idle hands, and soon after we arrived she handed each of us a basket and told us to pick currants in the garden. Smoothing out her large apron with her work-worn hands, as was her habit, she told us sternly to choose only ripe ones and not to crush the delicate berries when snipping them off. The day was sunny and bright. Her garden was splendidly colorful—a profusion of red and yellow flowers, faint-red ripening tomatoes, luscious green cucumber vines, and tall bushes with pale gooseberries, dark blackberries, and red currants. Rosy peaches were still ripening on trees, as were green apples and yellow pears. Flecked butterflies fluttered in the clear air and bees buzzed among sweet-smelling blossoms. In her garden, where all was quiet and peaceful, birds sang their happy, undisturbed songs and were answered by others, farther away. Korpantowa's garden was orderly, filled with beauty but also with vegetables and fruit needed for every day, as was our less spectacular garden. Her garden that day, which I remember so clearly despite the passage of time, seemed of another world, far away from the turmoil and weeping brought on by Grandmother Mindel's death.

Had I been alone I might have pretended to be in an enchanted garden, but Cousin Esther was standing on the other side of the berry bush and she had chosen this occasion to tell me about death. As always, her straight brown hair hung limply around her pale, freckled face. Since she was rather afraid of Korpantowa, she was picking the currants as carefully as we had been ordered. Memory has ways of embellishing events, yet for me that sunny day in the garden, when time seemed to stand still, is forever joined to the first seeds of doubt. At first we neither spoke nor quarreled. Silently we set to filling the baskets, here and there tasting some ripe berries. We heard the reassuring song of birds; we heard the clutter of dishes through Korpantowa's kitchen window; occasionally we heard her dog growl on his long chain in front of the house. The silence between us became oppressive, and rather to make conversation than to gather information I asked Cousin Esther if she thought that when the Messiah came Grandmother Mindel from the new cemetery would meet up with Grandfather Hayim, Great-grandfather Israel, and Great-grandmother Blime (after whom I was named) from the old cemetery. Her answer left no doubt. There is no Messiah and no going to the Holy Land, she said. The dead are dead and buried. Their hair and nails continue to grow a little longer in the grave; meanwhile worms eat their flesh until nothing remains but dry bones.

I remember the anger I always felt when Cousin Esther tried to humiliate me by letting me know she had access to superior knowledge. True, she went to the Polish school and studied subjects unlike those taught in my religious school, where instruction was confined to the Old Testament, selected commentaries, prayers, and large doses of Hebrew grammar. But usually it was Cousin Esther's sharp and nasty way of speaking, especially when she wanted to impress me with how much she knew, that caused my anger. Perhaps she also liked to see me get angry—as I, predictably, always did.

But this time it was different. The mention of worms had planted a seed of doubt in my tidy and familiar world. In my life there were all sorts of fearsome worms: the disgusting maggots in the outhouse; glistening reddish-brown earthworms in the vegetable garden; fat white worms one dreaded to come upon in cabbages; and, above all, the much-feared intestinal tapeworm that the older cousins forever reminded us younger ones to beware of, though how not to get it was left unsaid. I could not possibly accept what Cousin Esther was telling me, for the two images—Grandmother and worms—were incongruous, contrary, incomprehensible. And if nothing remained of the dead but dry bones, what was the point of the bag of soil from the Holy Land? What was the point of even thinking of the coming of the Messiah? That summer day in a garden filled with nature's abundance, with the wonders nature was able to bring forth from trees, soil, and shrubs, Cousin Esther taught me the lesson of life and death, of impermanence and decay, a lesson I was neither ready to hear nor able to understand just yet.

Who might we have become, Esther and I, had we remained in Mielec, grown old together? Would she have become like my aunt Feige, harsh and domineering? Or would she finally have learned to dream, and would I have liked her better then? But Cousin

Esther never had the chance—she was killed, and now she lives in my memory only as someone who rejected illusions, who faced reality as she understood it. Beneath the remembered harshness, she was, I think today, after all quite fragile.

When the seven days of mourning were over, life returned to its customary rhythms. Father and Uncle Reuven reopened the store, my father quite visibly sad. I missed hearing him hum his favorite tune, about Zion in the green fields, the pasture of little lambs. We again ate hot meals at noon, and everyone seemed to take it for granted that Grandmother was no longer around. But I couldn't stop brooding about her death. Nor did I forget Cousin Esther's words about the worms.

The first time I went to Grandmother's house after she died, I couldn't imagine her not being downstairs in the store, standing behind the counter checking the money in the drawer, or upstairs, at the stove, cooking one of her strong-smelling chicken soups. In fact, when I went inside I was sure I saw her standing in the shaft of sunlight from the open door, watching the busy street where peasants drove their wagons to market and women ambled by on errands. I thought she was wearing her long black wool skirt and, in spite of the warm weather, had a dark shawl around her shoulders. On her head was the hideous yellow wig, as usual slightly askew, for she was in the habit of scratching her head, pushing the wig over one ear. The small eyes in the wrinkled, sallow face were alert; were I to reach for a piece of candy in the big jar, I thought, she would surely see it. In life she had no teeth, and this made her nose look longer than it actually was and gave her face a perpetually discontented expression. Today, however, she smiled pleasantly. I rubbed my eyes and when I looked again she had disappeared. In her place stood Uncle Reuven in the dirty white coat he always wore when working in the store. On his face was the familiar sleepy, self-absorbed expression.

Had I "seen" Grandmother only this once after her death I might have forgotten all about it. The trouble was that I kept seeing her in various places around the house, upstairs in the morning at the kitchen table pounding chicory and coffee beans in the brass mortar; sitting up in the bed that stood in the left-hand corner of the kitchen, her toothless mouth open in an enormous yawn. The strange thing was that she was always very friendly, trying to give me something, which she had never done before. But each time, as soon as I stopped to look, she vanished. Grandmother appeared to me only in her own house, in the store downstairs or the apartment upstairs. I never saw her at, say, the bakery where I bought shiny, twisted bagels for breakfast, and where I brought the cholent Friday afternoons for baking overnight. Nor did I see her in Mordche's delicatessen, where Mother sometimes bought a crunchy cream-filled pastry for me.

Grandmother also did not appear when neighbors and relatives dropped by for afternoon chats. It had been their custom while Grandmother was alive and they continued to gather after she died. There would be five or six women, drinking lemonade and eating chickpeas, Hava with Hayim-Yankel invariably among them. Cousin Esther, the boy, and I sat on the threadbare green sofa that stood wedged between the window and the kitchen table, the broken springs digging into our skinny buttocks. We pretended to string beads, or to crochet, all the time trying not to miss a word of the women's talk.

Was it then that I heard this story I am about to tell, perhaps from Hava or by eavesdropping on the women's talk? Or maybe I read it later and memory somehow wove it into the fabric of Grandmother's death and my visualization of her, which I never confided to anyone. Perhaps I felt a child's guilt for not having liked her when she was alive, for being jealous when she bought sweet oranges for Cousin Esther and not for me. In any event, I came to learn that after a person dies the soul cannot free itself at once from the body. The seven days of mourning and the men's daily prayer in the mourner's house are to comfort the soul when it returns home during those days. It wanders back and forth between the grave and its erstwhile home until the seven days are over. Thereafter, for the entire year, the soul still continues between the grave and the sky; only after the year has passed will it remain permanently in heaven, though it may occasionally still visit the grave. That Grandmother Mindel could not rest in her grave and try to become accustomed to her place in heaven may have been due to something troubling her. Her soul was trying to give a sign that she was uneasy; perhaps she wanted to undo something she had done. Or maybe it was a matter of something she had failed to attend to and she wanted to let the family know that it ought to be done. Her restless soul ceased its visits shortly before war broke out. Never having told anyone about them, I soon forgot I had ever seen her after she died.

The rumors of war upset everyone. The entire family, including the side on the Small Market, was in a panic. Should we pack up and flee, or stay where we were? Would the Polish army make a stand at the Wisłoka River and blow up the bridge? Would Mielec become a battleground as it had in World War I between the Russian and Austrian armies, an event still remembered by many? Should we put in provisions for a long siege, or hope for a quick end to battles? Sleepy Mielec (though it had a railroad station and was a market town) was important to both the Polish and German armies because it had a bridge over which armies could retreat as well as invade. And then there was the nearby aircraft factory with its hangars and small airfield. Fears of war were not unfounded. Mielec, in its own way, had strategic significance.

Aunt Feige worried about looters. Before locking the store's iron shutters with the once so hotly contested key, she carried a large bag of ground chocolate to our house for safekeeping. Father was sure that the Germans would bomb the nearby aircraft factory, and that the impact could shatter our windowpanes. He cut up strips of paper and mixed flour and water to glue the strips over the glass. The Polish landlord was certain that his fine, two-story brick house would burn down. His face streaming with perspiration, he warned us not to light cooking fires once the war started.

Everyone was tense. People stopped one another on street corners to ask for the latest news. Father brought out the large radio—there weren't many in Mielec—which he usually stored in the attic because we had no place for it in our small room. He and I listened intently to the crackling and humming and were none the wiser. I ran over to Grandmother's house to say good-bye to Cousin Esther. Once war started, Mother had told me, I would not be allowed outside. This was no time to pursue old quarrels and I decided to ask Cousin Esther about war, since neither Father nor Mother seemed to be in the mood to answer questions.

I had only the haziest notion of what to expect. I knew about the biblical wars—those with the Amalekites, the Philistines, the Canaanites, not to mention the Assyrians and the Babylonians who destroyed the Holy Temple—but they had taken place so long ago. In our attic I had found a dusty old book about Napoléon's wars; the gory pictures of grim-faced soldiers lighting fires to cannons, while fountains of blood spurted from the bellies of soldiers lying on the ground, mesmerized me. Such reading was forbidden, and I had not told Mother about my find. Then there were stories the women told in Grandmother's kitchen about that earlier war when Grandmother Mindel and Great-grandmother Blime fled to Vienna, and when Father was sent to Holland to avoid being drafted into the Austrian army. There were also the songs we sang about war, learned heaven only knows where. We sang in Yiddish: "My name is Yossel Baer, and I serve in the army." Or the song in Polish about the uhlan who falls dead from his horse and is admonished by his comrades to dream about Poland in his dark grave. None of these bits and pieces of information, I felt, helped me understand.

Cousin Esther, for once, was thoughtful, even kind, as she explained things to me. Rubbing her yellow teeth, she said that first German airplanes would drop bombs. The bombs would explode with a terrible noise, and I must be sure to cover my ears, otherwise I would be deaf for the rest of my life. After the airplanes would come soldiers with machine guns. From them we had to hide. But, said Cousin Esther, the war would not last very long because the Polish army was small and weak and could not resist the superior German army.

One sunny afternoon, Hava came rushing over, her red-flowered shawl streaming behind her. Pale little Hayim-Yankel could barely keep up on his short, skinny legs. Hava looked more wild-eyed than ever and apparently had upsetting news. It turned out that she had heard that some Kabbalists were attempting to foretell the shape of things to come. They were otherworldly men, skilled in the use of numerology, who seldom read newspapers and never listened to the radio. However, in the tense days before the invasion of Poland, when no news at all came our way, least of all on the radio, the search for news by other means did not seem incongruous. Although reluctantly, even Father consented to hear Hava out. The gist of the Kabbalists' deliberations was (as I reconstructed with some help much later) that when the numerical values of the Hebrew letters for "Adolf," "Hitler," and "Mielic" are added, the sum total is 705. Now, the numbers 7, 0, and 5 correspond to the Hebrew letters *tav, shin,* and *hey,* and these, in turn, are the numbers in 1945. When the Hebrew letters are read as a word, its meaning is "exhausted" or "feeble."

The interpretation of the Kabbalists, as Hava understood it, was that Jews could expect terrible calamities until 1945. These calamities would leave them exhausted and ruined. The Kabbalists advised fleeing without delay, as fast and as far as possible. Thinking about it now, I imagine how Hava, hugging Hayim-Yankel, must have sobbed. Where was she, a woman alone with a small child, to go? And what were these terrible calamities we needed to fear?

No one paid attention to the Kabbalists' prophecy of doom, and no one followed their advice. That Hava did not flee is not surprising. But neither did the Kabbalists leave town, and people, no doubt, smiled indulgently, as did Father, at the hocus-pocus of numbers and Hebrew letters of a few old men.

JANUARY 1996

I like to teach my seminars at the Hebrew University in Jerusalem in the round room. I have only a handful of students. They too like this room with its soft light from the domed skylight and its suggestive remoteness, somehow appropriate to the subject I teach there, Chinese literature. It is not one of the popular courses. Most of today's students prefer practical lessons: politics, the booming Chinese economy, the one-party system. They boast of never having read Chinese fiction or poetry.

The students sitting in the round room, however, are dedicated readers. The one or two among them who take this course merely because it fits into their schedules are not disruptive. They are bored and stifle yawns, valiantly trying not to fall asleep. We are reading *The Dream of the Red Chamber,* an eighteenth-century Chinese novel that is one of the great masterpieces of world literature, even if the world has been slow to acknowledge it as such. It is a long novel, hundreds of pages, with plots and subplots and layers of meanings.

We have discovered that the concerns of the large and bewildering cast of characters are not extraordinary. They, and the hero and heroine of the tale, search as do we for the meaning of life and death, destiny, and an answer to the question of whether human beings can intervene in fate, change it from its apparently determined course. Time and again, the author wants his readers to understand the nature of human ignorance: our inability to recognize the signs, the road signs that indicate where we are headed but that we strangely don't seem to see. *The Dream,* as I like to call it, tells much about the ways human beings act in China and everywhere else. But the novel and its profound messages are not easily understood. Westerners express such matters differently. Even if we too speak of the riddle that living and dying is, we bring to it different perspectives, not all that dissimilar from the blind men who touch the trunk or foot of the elephant and think it is the entire animal. Ignorance prevents us from recognizing that we cannot apprehend reality.

Both the hero, Baoyu, and the heroine, Daiyu, are flawed, I explain, as they must be in an imperfect world. They are flawed despite their beginnings in the perfect, the mythic world, where they received their spiritual endowment. Baoyu was a stone who was rejected when the dome of heaven was built because he did not quite fit. As a result he developed a yearning for existence in the here and now. Daiyu's beginnings, also in the mythic world, were as a flower. But she too lacks perfection because she was lonely. Thus, the two, destined yet not destined for each other, and with their spiritual endowments of stone and flower, are born into this imperfect world.

The author of *The Dream* was from the south of China with its lush, green landscape of rivers and lakes. His family, once wealthy and respected, was impoverished by the time he began writing the novel, and he lived in straitened circumstances in the vastly different, northern capital of Beijing. The novel contains his youthful memories of the south, and a portion of the plot takes place in a garden with wonderful vegetation, sheltered from the turmoil of the outside world and its strife. Baoyu, Daiyu, and their teenage companions come to live in the garden, spending their days in innocent games and delighting in one another's company. But one by one, the young maidens must leave the garden to meet tragic fates outside: sickness, loveless and brutalizing marriages, and death. The girls are fragile, like the blossoms on the flowering trees; their youth is as ephemeral as the flowers that bloom with magnificent splendor and soon wilt.

At the height of their happiness and their families' wealth and status, the signs of decay and decline, including the signs of the youngsters' eventual destinies, are already present, I tell my students. When Baoyu dreams of reading the registers of their lives, he doesn't understand the words. In the riddle games the youngsters play, in which the older family members participate, the signs are in the riddles' answers. Yet neither old nor young relate the answers to their own lives.

Is it not the same with us, I ask, that we listen and don't hear, look and don't see? We are endowed with these capacities—the potential is contained in our spiritual beginnings—but we make no use of them. Our time in the garden of innocence, of sweet-smelling blossoms, of many-hued flowers, of wondrous birds, is ever so brief. Soon we must leave the garden, which, with no one to tend it, falls into neglect, decays. We are shown the means of changing our destinies, and yet we don't make use of them. The students look skeptical. Some things cannot be changed, they argue. This is not how they see the world. They believe they have never been in childhood's magic garden, and they don't think they have ever seen signposts of things to come.

The war, when it broke out, seemed at first far away. But it brought a strange silence to Mielec. Life seemed to have come to a halt. The peasants' wagons no longer rumbled to market. Stores were barred and bolted. Shoppers dashed through back doors and quickly rushed home again. The bakers still baked bread, but behind closed doors. Mothers kept their children at home, and in the late afternoon people no longer visited back and forth as had been their custom. All was quiet. Everyone waited while the sun shone in the cloudless sky. The days were beautiful and bright, filled with delicious smells of flowers and late-ripening fruit in our garden. Earthworms were busy in the cabbage patch and large butterflies trembled on the apple tree.

Not being allowed out of the garden, I was bored. Worry mixed with fear created an oppressive heaviness in the household, so I went down into the garden with my book and sat in the shade of the large walnut tree. Our garden—actually the landlord's—was not like Korpantowa's. It had fruit trees and vegetables, but neither the landlord nor the other families living in the house had planted berry shrubs. But I liked sitting under the walnut tree; I liked watching the sun and drifting clouds through the dense foliage; I even liked the apprehensive waiting for the caterpillars that occasionally dropped on my hands or neck. I read about Samson and Delilah, about love and betrayal, about the heavy price of blind love and trust. I read about King David and his son Absalom, as I had many times before, and I thought again how deeply David loved this son though he betrayed his father's love. "Absalom, my son, my son, Absalom," sobbed David when the messenger brought the news of his death. David's bitter lament and the sadness of love, betrayal, and death never failed to bring tears to my eyes.

One day while I was in the garden I heard a noise, not exactly a noise, more like a loud silence of a kind I had never heard before. I hurried upstairs. We were all standing on the balcony of Aunt Sheindl's room when we saw the retreating Polish army. The weary soldiers in their torn and grimy uniforms shuffled down the street raising clouds of dust. Their heads were bowed, they spoke in barely audible voices, they were listless—a beaten army. They were also barefoot, and Mother said it was because their shoes had been made of paper that dissolved in the rain. She had a compassionate heart and so she went downstairs to draw water from the well for the tired soldiers. Father believed that the Germans were already nearby. But since the Polish army apparently did not plan to make a stand at the Wisłoka River, bringing the front to our doorsteps, we had nothing to fear, according to Father.

Another day we stood on the balcony and watched a silver airplane in the cloudless sky, not knowing whether it was German or Polish. We seemed to have quite forgotten to go down into the cellar at the sight of airplanes, as we had been told. The airplane circled once, twice, and then disappeared. We heard two loud crashes that shook the house. That was all. Father's taped windows did not break, nor had the bridge over the river been bombed. The Germans needed the bridge to march over it into Mielec. We later learned that the noise had been made by bombs falling on or near the aircraft factory.

Like spectators in a theater, we stood yet another time on the balcony watching the refugees streaming into town. Men and women, old and young, they carried a few pitiful belongings on their backs or had packed them high onto handcarts. They too raised great clouds of dust, but unlike the soldiers, they did not leave. The refugees had come to stay, thinking it perhaps safer in town than in the open country. Mother again went downstairs to draw water for the frightened and exhausted people and to find out how close the German army was.

Now the streets were no longer silent. Dust-covered men and women wandered up and down the alleys, knocking on shuttered windows and doors. They begged to buy bread and some milk, and they begged to be given shelter, while tiny babies wailed loudly in their mothers' arms. Our landlord stood guard at the gate and would not allow anyone into the garden. They are thieves waiting only for a chance to steal, he said. Father thought that once the Germans came the war would be over for us. I very much wanted to believe him.

In September, on the eve of the Jewish New Year, the Germans' motorcycles roared into town. They came on the same road as the Polish army and the refugees. There were not many Germans, I seem to remember, but there were enough to accomplish what they had come to do. We stood on the balcony watching the motorcycles, listening to the unaccustomed, sinister sounds. We may have been relieved at first that a battle had not taken place near or in Mielec. We may have been apprehensive, wondering what these German conquerors might do in town. We did not know then as we watched from the balcony that they came for one purpose only: to murder Jews.

Preparations for the holiday had not been elaborate that year. Due to the outbreak of war, there had been no weekly markets, and peasants from nearby villages brought neither fruit nor vegetables. Still, the Mielec Jews felt that the worst was over. The Polish army had crumbled, the Germans were conquering Poland, but life goes on; holidays—the holiest of the yearly cycle—must be observed as best one could. People cooked whatever they had.

Others who had managed to fatten a chicken or goose through the weeks of tension brought it in the morning to the butcher for the ritual slaughter. Ritual ablutions are especially important in festival observance, and while the women prepared the household for the holiday, the men prepared their bodies and minds. The bathhouse was unusually crowded that day, both because of the importance of religious bathing and because the many refugees in town simply needed to bathe.

After the Germans had roared into town on their motorcycles they surrounded the bathhouse and the butcher shop. The men from the former were herded into the latter; Jews passing by, or heading toward the bathhouse, easily recognizable by their beards, earlocks, and clothing, were also caught and driven into the butcher shop. Except for women and children, who were sent home, no one was allowed to escape. The Germans then either shot the people dead, setting fire to the buildings afterward, or set fire to the buildings then and there and burned the people alive. Accounts differ. No reporter was present to set down the facts and the sequence of events. And if anyone immediately thereafter recorded in a diary what happened (as someone well may have), the diary is long since lost, destroyed as was not much later Jewish Mielec and most of its people.

After killing the people at the butcher shop and setting fire to the Jewish section, the Germans went to the synagogue (some said later that the Germans had gone but returned on the eve of the Day of Atonement) to set it on fire. First they made a large bonfire with prayer books, Torah scrolls, and other books from the houses of study that adjoined each side of the synagogue. The synagogue was a large stone edifice with two round turrets; it stood back from the street and had a forecourt that was convenient for the book burning. The houses of study were built of wood, which the flying sparks quickly ignited; the raging fire then spread to the synagogue. Late at night, after their work was done, the Germans left; or perhaps only some left, because on the morning after, the Jews were prevented from burying the dead in the new cemetery.

What happened in Mielec that day is always told briefly by historians. And in the telling, the events of that New Year's Eve are neutralized, stripped of the horror of an endless day and an endless night. Nearly fifty years after the event, one historian wrote: "At Mielec, on September 13, thirty-five Jews were arrested in the communal baths, taken to the slaughterhouse, and then burned alive. Another twenty were burned alive in the synagogue." A Polish historian, in a book of more than a thousand pages about Mielec and its surroundings, merely remarks: "Already in September 1939, the Germans in Mielec burned down the synagogue together with several dozen Jews. All died." Compared to what took place in the years thereafter, what happened on the eve of the holiday may be seen as insignificant, not deserving larger mention. Besides, the pogroms, as we came to call them, were carried out in other towns as well; few were spared. Yet how easily the eye fails to register the brief sentences. How effortlessly the reader moves on to other events, in which thousands and millions perished. Only several dozen Jews? A synagogue burned down? The bathhouse? Barely worth the reader's attention. These brief sentences about Mielec will quite likely become even briefer and may one day vanish altogether from history. Questions remain that may never be answered. Who were these faceless Germans in their gray uniforms and large helmets who successfully practiced their first mass murder? Were they soldiers in the German Tenth Army, which operated in this part of Poland? Were they part of the "motorized regiment" of the SS, attached to the Tenth Army, which after Mielec went on to massacre Jews elsewhere? And was the commander of the Tenth Army, Walter

von Reichenau, indeed outraged when he learned of the SS
doings?

We stood on the balcony and heard the terrible screams. The
house we lived in was on the very edge of the Polish section, separated from the Jewish part of town by only a large field. On the
other side of the field were two or three apartment houses, the
bakery, and some shops. Next to those stood the large bathhouse
and, perpendicular to it, the butcher shop. The inhuman screams
of people dying carried through the clear air, but we did not know
what they meant.

We smelled the smoke, the smoke of burning wood and burning flesh, and did not know what that meant either. Then we saw
the fire. A wall of flames slowly engulfed the street in front of us.
We heard shots, mad laughter, and terror-stricken shrieks, and we
knew then that a portion of the Jewish part of town was in flames.
The Polish landlord ran up the stairs together with his hard-faced
wife, who carried their twin daughters. He shouted at us to leave:
If the Germans discovered that he had Jewish tenants they would
surely set fire to his house as well. We obeyed meekly and he, caring only for his house, watched us go, while his two little daughters, wide-eyed, each clutched one of his legs.

Quietly we made our way through the garden and out a back
gate into the large potato field. It was still a month or more
before the harvest and the green, sturdy stalks stood high and
dense. We did not dare go into the street; we did not know where
to go. Father decided that we must stay in the potato field until
morning.

Throughout that long summer night, I heard the red fire roar
and felt hot gusts of wind on my face. I saw showers of sparks
shoot up into the sky. I thought I saw terrible monsters with

machine guns advance toward me through the fence. I pressed my body deep into the soft earth, praying for the potato plants to hide me and my family. The earth smelled damp and fresh, but I choked in the smoke-filled air. Red clouds of smoke drifted through the night. The world was on fire with everything and everybody in it. I covered my ears, but in the roar of the fire I still thought I heard the terrible shrieks and the mad laughter. As I pressed my body into the black earth that night I was possessed by an unerasable fear of death that for many years to come would have a place in my memory. Inarticulately, it would surface time and again, paralyzing, immobilizing, and overcoming the rational person. A fear that had the sound of a thousand shrieks, an unsharable fear that was mine alone. Only many years later was I able to find a place for this fear among much else that must not be forgotten.

When at last day dawned gray and damp, we crept back through the gate into the garden and upstairs to our apartment. Again I stood on the balcony. I looked down into the street that led past the bakery to the bathhouse and the butcher shop. All the houses were in ruin as far as the eye could see. Like great red fingers, chimneys pointed starkly into the gray, sunless sky— especially the large chimney of the bakery, where only a few weeks ago we had bought blueberry cakes called *kikerlech.* The beams of the houses closest to ours still smoldered and thin wisps of smoke hung motionless above the ruins. The heavy morning air seemed to have trapped the pungent smell of the great fire. Down below, in the garden, the trees were covered with fine gray ash. A strange, oppressive silence hung over this dead scene. Even the birds had fled from the garden. Cocks did not crow, nor did hens cackle. None of the customary morning sounds were to be heard.

I remember seeing people beginning to arrive in the backyard of the charred house on the other side of the field. Several men came with shovels and hurriedly started digging a large pit.

Although there was no sun, the day was turning hot and sultry, and the diggers stopped frequently to wipe their foreheads. Other men crowded into the yard bringing bundles that they gingerly put on the ground at some distance from the pit. They gestured to one another silently; they neither wept nor moaned. The silent crowd watched the silent diggers. When the pit was dug, the men carefully placed the bundles in it, one by one. They chanted a barely audible prayer, quickly filled in the pit, and hurried out into the street.

I watched without understanding. I was hypnotized by the silent drama taking place below, unable to tear myself away, yet knowing that something terrible, unfathomable, was happening. A picture was implanted that was never to be erased, that remained as vivid nearly sixty years later as on that overcast morning. Perhaps it was Mother or Father who eventually explained. Or perhaps I overheard others talking. Only in time would I understand what I had seen, which was that all morning pious men from the burial society had carefully collected charred bodies and bones. Most victims were burned beyond recognition; there was no way of knowing who they were, who was a stranger and who a townsman, or which shoulder bone belonged with which skull. Why the backyard of this particular house was selected for the burial, or why it was decided to bury the charred remains in a mass grave there, was never mentioned.

In the weeks that followed I tried not to look in the direction of the pit, its outline clearly visible from the balcony. The memory of what I had seen that morning continued to haunt me, bringing a new kind of fear. What if the Germans had found us in the potato field and we too had been consumed by the roaring fire? Would I now be a bundle of charred bones, unrecognizable, with no face? And what would have happened to my soul, would it be roaming about (I still halfheartedly believed it would travel despite Cousin

Esther's blunt explanation), unable to recognize my charred bones or, worse yet, would it mistake someone else's for mine? I thought of Grandmother Mindel and how I had imagined her lying peacefully in her very own grave, perhaps wearing the gray Sabbath wig, instead of the everyday yellow one, waiting, waiting. . . . And I thought of the bundles of charred bones in the pit after the night of terror, and of the roar of the fire, and of the unearthly shrieks.

The garden began to have that end-of-summer look. The leaves on the cucumber vines turned dry and dusty. The bean stalks drooped without their shiny, heavy pods, and the apple trees, after the landlord picked the fruit, were left not exactly barren, but somehow lacking fullness. The potato field that adjoined the garden was no longer a sea of lush green leaves, shimmering in the sun. The high stalks that had hidden us during the pogrom were turning a dull brown. Soon they would wither and drop to the ground, and then women and children would swarm over the field to dig the potatoes out of the rich, dark soil.

I was not allowed to leave the garden, and I had no intention of doing so anyway. In the garden I felt safe. I sat under the large walnut tree, its crown increasingly sparse. Throughout the summer, the fat, weirdly cold caterpillars had dropped down, but at the first sign of autumn they had vanished. I now missed them and the pleasant apprehension I had felt then. Without the Feast of Tabernacles there had been no transition to autumn. Neither Father nor anyone else had built the traditional booth. The passage of time had lost its landmarks. Cracks were appearing in my tidy world. If Father regretted his promise to Grandmother Mindel not to split up the family, there was nothing he could do about it now. And within a year it would be too late.

From an administrative circular, November 23, 1940:

I empower you to reject unconditionally all requests for emigration . . . because emigration from the General Government is . . . no
longer permitted. . . . [nor may] a Jew receive a travel pass . . . to
request a visa from a foreign consulate in Germany.

One day I took out my schoolbooks and sat on the balcony,
intending to read. But I couldn't keep my mind on the stories. My
eyes strayed beyond the garden to the blackened remains of the
houses and the outline of the pit. White, fleecy clouds obscured
the sun and a sudden chill was in the air. As shadows appeared,
the blackened ruins across the field looked menacing. How was I
to grasp the terrible dying that had occurred? How was the Messiah to lead charred bones to the Holy Land? Was there perhaps
no Messiah after all? Was there no waiting in graves? Was Cousin
Esther right that in the end only bones remained in the earth? I
relived the night of terror, of red flames reaching into the sky.
Fears swept over me, fears without words.

Suddenly, there were many uncertainties. The world that had
been a known place, of one piece, ordered and orderly, now had
fissures, matters no longer known. Was Grandmother already
devoured by worms? How was it, how could it be, that living
human beings became charred bones? I could not put it into
words, I only felt somehow, wordlessly, as children do, that nothing could ever be the same again.

When winter came, a pure white blanket of snow would cover
the outlines of the pit with its charred bones and I would
no longer be reminded of the bundles buried there. The ruined
houses, their jagged outlines softened by the snow, would still line
the street, but I would avoid them by making a wide detour when
going to Grandmother's house.

Other things began to occupy me as time went by. Everyone and everything was changing in hard-to-comprehend ways. And I too was changing, becoming skinnier and taller and developing an enormous appetite for foods no longer to be had. Only Cousin Esther remained as quarrelsome as ever, although her sneers no longer bothered me because I had found a new friend, Tośka, a refugee from Kraków. Hava stopped visiting us. She had become very strange, Mother said, and was seen talking to herself in the street. I still occasionally saw her with Hayim-Yankel, her gray hair wilder than ever. She did not seem to recognize me and I did not approach her. She increasingly resembled the madwoman who lived at the corner of the Small Market.

Although I would be granted a little longer to dream in the garden of childhood, the time of endings had already arrived. The time of endings of Father's songs, which only he knew.

CHAPTER FOUR

TOŚKA

Flowing water, falling flowers
Spring is gone
In heaven as on earth.

LI YÜ (937–978)

Behind me, I don't see the ancients.
Ahead of me, I don't see those who came.
Thinking of limitless, endless heaven and earth
In solitary sorrow my tears fall.

CHEN ZI'ANG (661–702)

Tośka Spyrina, her parents, and her elder sister were refugees from Kraków. Her father had been a journalist there. In Mielec he was seldom at home. Her mother was very beautiful. She had black, almond-shaped eyes, an olive complexion, and shiny black hair. Tośka had her father's blue eyes and brown curly hair. She and her family were killed in Bełżec. I had a friend. Her name was Tośka. She was killed in Bełżec.

Our friendship was brief, lasting barely two years, yet I have never ceased mourning for Tośka. I last saw her perhaps a day or two before we were deported from Mielec, and then she and her family vanished, together with the many thousands. The story of our friendship exists as fragments in my memory, fragmented scenes that are connected to people around us we found interesting, or the secret school we attended for a time. I no longer know if we then felt the impermanence of our friendship. But I do know that the life of imagination that we shared knew neither time nor its limitations.

Shortly after the great fire, but before the Germans seized control of Mielec, life gradually and ever so cautiously took on a certain familiar rhythm. Yet the familiarity was deceptive, untrustworthy, and fear continued to hover like a giant shadow over the streets where the Jews lived. We could not avoid the German soldiers in their gray uniforms who came and went and who were a constant reminder of what they were capable of doing. There was also the Gestapo headquarters on a busy thoroughfare not far from the Small Market, which we called "the Gestapo house." I was convinced that it contained untold dangers, that it was the house where people were tortured for whatever crimes the Gestapo thought they had committed.

Then some men began disappearing; sometimes whole families. Their houses stood empty, doors locked securely, and within them, deserted and abandoned, were the possessions accumulated over a lifetime. Where had the people gone? Would they return? One day the entire Friedman family, who lived across from Grandmother Mindel's store, was gone—the old couple, their many sons and the sons' wives, the little grandchildren. Even the youngest son, who had the habit of running away from home, only to be found and brought back by one of his brothers a few days later (on one such occasion, to the family's shame, he had cut off his earlocks), had disappeared. All was quiet across the street as I looked down from Grandmother Mindel's upstairs apartment. I didn't understand what was happening; even the half-overheard hurried conversations didn't provide a clue to me.

But one day, with the sadness of autumn and the smell of roasting potatoes already in the air, the mystery was solved. Early one evening a group of men had gathered in our tiny room. There were Father, Uncle Reuven, Dr. Seiden (the dentist), and Mr. Feiner and his daughter's handsome fiancé. They had come to discuss escape to the Russian-occupied part of Poland. The door to our relatives' room was firmly closed. Uncle did not approve of these discussions and wanted no part in the escape plot. I sat in my customary corner, the small space between the wardrobe and the door, with the bookcase and its forbidden treasures, the books only the adults were supposed to read, behind me. Though I was half hidden, I could see the men's worried faces in the dim lamp-light.

They spoke one by one, keeping their voices low. They would have to cross—perhaps even swim—the Bug River to reach the Russian side. But how wide was the river? Would they be able to rent a boat? They did not know how far Mielec was from the Bug, what the roads were like, whether they should go by train, or whether it was safer to take a Polish peasant and wagon. They were afraid of German patrols. What if they were stopped by the Germans? Doctor Seiden had brought a map, which he spread on the shiny brass table where we sometimes played rummy. The men moved their heads close together, trying to find Mielec and the Bug on the small map in the dim light of the flickering oil lamp. As was his custom, Uncle Reuven tipped his hat back so that it nearly fell off his head.

Now a new question arose: Should they take their families along, and if so, how would the women and children manage the crossing? Uncle Reuven was for leaving the families behind. Men were in greater danger than women, he argued; Father seemed to

agree with him, saying that deep down the Germans were sufficiently civilized not to harm women and children. In the great
fire, they didn't burn women and children, only men. But Dr. Seiden, who had a measure of authority because he was a dentist,
insisted that everyone was in danger from the Germans. How civilized are people who set fires and kill men who meant them no
harm? he asked. He shook his head. Nothing good could be
expected from them, Jews must beware.

They argued back and forth and I, in my corner, now understood what the disappearance of the Friedmans and the others
meant. But understanding brought new fears. Could Father be
thinking of leaving us behind? What would we do without him?
We needed him to protect us from the Germans. What would we
do if he were suddenly to disappear, as had the others? (I didn't
know then of Father's promise to Grandmother Mindel that he
would never split up the family.)

In the days thereafter the meeting no longer seemed as sinister.
Father was there as always and Uncle Reuven stood sleepily
behind the counter in the empty store. The days were bright and
sunny and I began to gather chestnuts to carve into small baskets,
to string for necklaces, and to make dolls, for which the chestnuts
were also strung together. Mr. Feiner, our neighbor, was often in
the yard helping his wife chop wood. He worked silently and
methodically, splitting each piece into several small ones. Mrs.
Feiner, brown-skinned and round, would hum a tune and care-
lessly split her kindling into thick and thin, crooked and straight
pieces.

The Feiners had moved into the small, whitewashed wooden
cottage where the Polish landlord had lived before he built the
two-story house into which he and we moved. The old, run-down
place had tiny windows, a heavy straw-covered roof, and, facing
the street, a small porch with two narrow benches. Mrs. Feiner

was a pleasant woman who smiled a great deal and sometimes sang while doing her work. She was not religious and did not wear a wig; her graying hair was always pulled back into a partially undone bun. Mr. Feiner was almost as dark-skinned as his wife. Although clean-shaven, he kept his head covered, as did most other so-called emancipated Jews. In contrast to his cheerful wife, he was sullen, rarely speaking with the other tenants.

The Feiners had a daughter, probably around eighteen years old, and a son who may have been fourteen. The son was as dark as his parents, with a mischievous face and a grin like his mother's. The daughter was very different: She was blonde and blue-eyed, with a fair, almost milky-white complexion; neither short nor tall, she wore high-wedged wooden sandals, each wedge painted a different color, as had become fashionable in summer when leather was no longer available. Her light print dresses of gauzy material billowed in the wind when she walked down the street. She was already engaged to be married (or so I assumed), and I often saw her on their front porch with her fiancé. They were a handsome couple, sitting on one of the narrow benches, gazing into each other's eyes, and discussing earnestly what, I was certain, were their wedding plans. The menacing reality of the recent past and the uncertainties of the present were perhaps more bearable for me, a ten-year-old, when I imagined romance and happy endings, like in the fairy tales I knew.

The warm, sunny days of early autumn soon gave way to rain and piercing winds, turning the unpaved streets into treacherous mud in which the peasants' horse-drawn carts left deep furrows. One needed to walk gingerly, avoiding puddles and thick slush in order not to lose one's precious and irreplaceable galoshes. During the summer, Mother had taken to knitting hats for the family with wool recycled from old sweaters. They were nothing fancy, merely a longish scarf sewn together perhaps one-quarter of its length to provide a one-piece hat and scarf. Her hats, with a pointed horn sticking up in back, were not in the least attractive, but they were serviceable and kept out the wind.

Although I hated the cold weather, I was restless that autumn, frightened that Father might suddenly vanish in the dark of night while I was asleep. My self-imposed task was to keep watch on him, going regularly to the store to make sure he and Uncle Reuven were there. Also, even if I was bound to quarrel with Cousin Esther, it was better to carve the chestnuts I had gathered in her company rather than alone at home, oppressed by gray clouds and incessant rain.

The Seidens were now gone. They had left their beautiful large house on the outskirts of Mielec to which in the past Mother and I were occasionally invited for afternoon tea. For me, and I think for Mother too, this had always been a grand affair: The two of us would dress in our best clothes. We might even take a droshke, the horse-drawn cabs only better-off people used. Riding in a droshke, I seem to remember, was done only on the most special occasions. Tea was ever so genteel; old Mrs. Seiden and Mother chatted politely, each balancing a delicate porcelain cup in one hand and holding a cookie in the other, while I was allowed to inspect the "winter garden." This was a glassed-in porch where Mrs. Seiden grew exotic plants—or at least they seemed exotic to my untrained eye. Now their house also stood empty and silent in the barren fields of the gray autumn. The plants, neglected, would soon wither and die.

The handsome fiancé of the Feiners' daughter and Mr. Feiner were also gone. I did not worry about how Mrs. Feiner would manage. She seemed quite capable, and as it turned out she did indeed get on very well. I was more concerned for her beautiful daughter, whether she would remain true to the handsome fiancé, whether he would forget her once he had crossed the faraway Bug.

The idea of crossing the Bug (it did not occur to me that one might also get to the Russian side without crossing the river) led me to wild imaginings: a dark moonless night; men, women, and children huddle tightly packed in a flimsy boat; Mr. Feiner and his daughter's fiancé frantically row across the Bug, which surely must be wider than our Wisłoka, where once an uncle tried to teach me how to swim and where I sank like a stone. Cousin Esther, who also did not know how to swim, had told me all about the dangers of the river, mentioning numerous cases of drowning here and elsewhere, including that of a girl named Ophelia who had been in love with a prince in faraway Denmark. Rivers were treacherous. I imagined Mrs. Friedman, in the fine black coat in which she had made her rounds of visits each afternoon, clutching the side of the boat, the crying babies next to her. I could well imagine how cold the river water would be in autumn. I can't remember sharing my anxieties with anyone, certainly not with Cousin Esther, who no doubt would have found reasons to ridicule me.

After Mr. Feiner left, Mrs. Feiner began to bake bread to sell in the neighborhood. Her loaves were large, black, and heavy and never quite round, which did not, however, deter anyone from buying them. Mother said Mrs. Feiner stretched the dough by adding potatoes. But all the same, she thought that Mrs. Feiner was very brave for finding ways of supporting her children. In her own quiet way, Mother tried to help Mrs. Feiner whenever she could.

Still, as time went by, Mother began to grow suspicious. Something was not quite right about Mrs. Feiner and her bread. Flour was rationed. Everyone we knew ate bread as sparingly as if it were cake. The Birnbaum bakery never had enough bread and was always short of flour. Yet Mrs. Feiner managed to get hold of flour. She and her curly-haired son, who helped deliver the bread, appeared regularly at our door. When no one else had bread, Mrs. Feiner could always be counted on. She came up our staircase, a cheerful smile on her round face, as if she didn't have a care in the world. Her son with his dancing black eyes was by her side. In religious school I had been taught not to look at boys, but I couldn't help stealing glances at this boy whose manner was so mischievous and forward.

Toward winter the first Jewish refugees, whom the Germans were deporting from the large cities, began arriving in Mielec. People squeezed still closer together and rented rooms to the newcomers. Some refugees arrived with only the clothes on their backs, others carried bundles and suitcases. A rabbi's wife with two small, whimpering children moved into Mrs. Feiner's two-room house. The rabbi's wife had a kerchief tightly wound around her head. She was pale and had pink eyes, which, oddly, were not framed by eyelashes. Being afraid of strangers, her children were always crying and hanging on to her skirts. I tried to play with them, but they just stared at me with big, frightened eyes and hid behind their mother. Throughout the long, cold winter I wondered how the three cheerful Feiners and this sad woman got along in the small cottage. When Mrs. Feiner was not delivering bread, she was baking it, her full brown arms up to the elbows in flour. The rabbi's wife never went out, except to buy food.

Mother often talked about the refugees. There being so little food and almost no wood or coal for cooking and heating, we were all badly off, said Mother, but for the refugees it was ten times worse. They had no money and for the most part no relatives in town. They were strangers with no one to help them in times of need. Mother had a compassionate heart and she even pitied the sad-faced, pink-eyed rabbi's wife and her two cranky children. Aunt Feige may have also pitied the refugees, but she was more practical. In her store few were given credit, and those who got it were usually people she knew.

Spring had not yet arrived in 1940 when I met Tośka. Where might I first have seen her? Would it have been when she and her mother came to the store? Often, after still another quarrel with Cousin Esther, I hid in the little room adjoining the store. This had been Great-grandmother Blime's room and was now used for storing odds and ends: barrels for making sauerkraut in the fall, buckets for carrying water, empty boxes, old rags. It had no windows and the only light came from the open door. Whenever I sat in that room, perhaps because I was named after Great-grandmother, I thought of her—wondering what she had been like, how she had looked, whether she had been happy or sad. Even though none of her possessions remained in the little room, I felt strangely close to her among the clutter, as if some substance of her, kindly and comforting, still remained. I had been told that unlike "modern" Grandmother Mindel, Great-grandmother Blime did not wear a wig but rather a white turban on which strands of pearls were sewn. After Great-grandmother Blime died—at the venerable age of ninety-nine, it was said— each of Grandmother Mindel's children received one of these strands. Father gave his to Mother, and whenever she wore it, I felt as if part of Great-grandmother was still with us.

If I had been in the little room when Tośka and her mother came in, I would have seen her at the counter when her mother paid. I might not have spoken to her just then, but I clearly remember that from the very first moment I saw Tośka I wanted her to be my friend. Perhaps it was she who spoke to me first; Tośka was a straightforward and unaffected person. However it happened, we became friends quickly and naturally, and my admiration for her grew the more I got to know her. She was only some months or at most a year older than I and wrote poetry, beautiful, wonderfully melodious verses. Our friendship-to-be was all too brief, yet while it lasted no disagreements marred it. It was as if we wanted to enjoy each other to the fullest. Was it that we sensed more keenly than did the adults the precariousness of our time of friendship?

To Tośka I confided the parting of the lovers, Mrs. Feiner's daughter and her fiancé, and she then began to talk about their reunion and marriage. The more we discussed the lovers the more extravagant our romantic notions became. Reality vanished. We built a fantasy world in which not only Mrs. Feiner's daughter and her fiancé existed, but we too had a place. Tośka was confident that, as in the fairy stories we knew, the fiancé would return, the war would end, and they would marry. They would fly into each other's arms, both as beautiful as they had been at their parting. She would blush, he would hold her hand and gently kiss her forehead. Mrs. Feiner, round and brown and with her arms covered in flour, would beam at the embarrassed couple. At the wedding the bride would wear a white lace gown, Tośka thought; she knew more about such matters than I. It would be spring and we would bring her a huge bouquet of spring flowers. Mrs. Feiner wouldn't bake bread any longer, she would bake a wedding cake with the finest white flour, and everyone would eat as many pieces as they wanted. After the wedding, the couple would leave in a carriage drawn by three white horses while five hundred wedding guests danced through the night.

But spring was a long way off. As we looked out the window, the houses seemed grayer than ever in the wintry air. Clouds heavy with snow covered the sky. On the ground, fresh snow was thick and white. The peasants rode their sleighs to town and we heard the faint ringing of the horses' bells. Their sound was melancholy. Tośka and I tried to imagine what spring would be like. Purple lilacs would cover the fence and the old chestnut tree would shimmer with white, candlelike blossoms. Sweet apple and cherry blossoms would appear on the landlord's fruit trees. If we were careful not to let him see us, we might pick some and suck their honey.

By the time spring actually came Tośka and I were inseparable. Now that the weather was warmer we spent more time outdoors, breathing the fresh air and turning our faces to the warming sun. The sun melted the ice around the well and little rivulets flowed through the yard toward the gate. The hard frozen earth of winter turned soft and steamy; it had a fragrance all its own. I listened to the first timid birdcalls and was relieved when the ugly black crows, whose mournful calls had frightened me, disappeared from their perch on the fence.

But spring brought more hunger. Except for Aunt Feige's family, everyone was eating their last provisions or had already finished them. Refugees continued to pour into Mielec and the little we had was stretched even more. I saw refugee children with swollen bellies and ugly sores. Mother said they had too much salt and acid in their little bodies from eating nothing but pickles. We were getting paler and thinner and were down to nearly the last of the potatoes stored in the cellar. The winter cabbage was almost finished as well, but Mother had saved a small supply of leaves that she tried to keep fresh. Although I had not eaten pickles, I had large painful boils full of pus on my arms and legs that the cabbage leaves were supposed to draw out.

Now I rarely went to Grandmother Mindel's house to play with Cousin Esther, and at times I felt guilty about neglecting her for my new friend. Cousin Esther appeared occasionally in my dreams, strangely changed, no longer rubbing her yellow teeth or calling me names. The dream Esther was much nicer, even prettier; she offered to share a piece of cake with me, she offered me an apple, she invited me to play a game of dominoes. Although I knew it was just a dream, I sometimes wondered whether the dream Esther was not more real than the one who taunted me. Memory may be playing tricks on me, for who can remember dreams of so long ago? Was I dreaming then, or later? What part was real, what part a dream? Or do I remember the dreams because I am ambivalent today, and guilty because of how I felt about Cousin Esther then? She never shared food with me when I was hungry and she never treated me very well. Yet, here I am, alive, able to eat my fill of cake and apples, while Esther is dead, shot dead by Rudi Zimmermann, the one whose parents bought provisions in Grandmother Mindel's store before war broke out and before he became a *Volksdeutscher*.

Mrs. Feiner continued to bake bread. Her prices had increased sharply and there were few customers for whole loaves. Her son no longer helped deliver the bread. Sliced into neat and carefully weighed wedges, it was packed in a big basket that she carried over her arm. I tried to be at home when Mrs. Feiner and her fragrant basket were expected. While I inhaled the sweet smell of freshly baked bread, Mother carefully chose a wedge. As usual, Mother asked whether Mrs. Feiner had heard from her husband. As always in recent months, Mrs. Feiner shrugged her shoulders. She was no longer as cheerful as she had been and, like others, was heard to say that those "on the other side" had already forgotten the families they left behind. Mother continued to wonder where Mrs. Feiner found potatoes and flour for her bread, and although my sister seemed to know something about that, she either did not want to tell Mother or did not want to tell her in front of me.

I saw Mrs. Feiner's daughter occasionally that spring. Whenever I heard the cheerful clatter of her wooden sandals on the brick walk to their cottage, I rushed to the gate to catch a glimpse of her. She didn't look as sad as I had imagined. In contrast to her mother, she looked happy, her blonde hair blowing in the soft spring breeze. At first Tośka and I were concerned. Could it be that the beautiful girl had forgotten her fiancé? Where was she going looking so happy and carefree? She was forcing herself to look cheerful, Tośka decided after much debate, she was being brave, showing the world that she believed in her beloved's return. Her fiancé when he returned was to see her laughing and rosy-cheeked, not pale and weeping.

As spring turned to summer we began to pay less attention to love and separation. Jewish children were no longer allowed to attend either Polish or Jewish schools, yet throughout the long winter neither Tośka nor I had really missed going to school. It had seemed a prolonged vacation, filled with our new friendship, the games we invented, the fantasies we spun. Between our real and imagined worlds, we were not bored, neither with one another nor for want of things to do. But then one day toward the end of spring we suddenly missed learning, missed the routine, missed doing homework. We also missed the freedom to roam. We wanted to be outside, in the warm sunshine, to glory in the smells of summer, feel the freshness of warm summer rains, drink in sounds and sights. Yet we didn't dare venture far from home. Our small world contained new dangers and Mother restricted us close to home. She no longer sent me and Cousin Esther to drink fresh goat's milk as she had in previous summers. I missed the walk to the goats through the ripening wheat fields. I would have liked to introduce Tośka to the crimson poppies and purplish blue cornflowers there. But it was too dangerous to go to the fields.

Tośka and I learned to be careful that summer. German soldiers were catching men and boys, sending them to the Pustkow labor camp. Our cousin Hayim, Shime-Duvid's son, whom I had admired because he had attended the Polish high school and had worn a "gymnasiast's" cap, was caught and sent there. Pustkow's guards were known for their brutality, and Shime-Duvid moved heaven and earth to get his son released, with no success. Only a few weeks later, Hayim was dead—beaten to death by a guard when he stepped aside to urinate. The Germans were even rounding up children in the streets to work in the fields; because of their nimble fingers the children were used to remove caterpillars from the ripening cabbages.

I learned to take back roads to Grandmother's store to avoid the large "Gestapo house" on the busy main thoroughfare. Tośka and I learned to be careful when Polish boys were nearby; they were known to throw stones, and they might beat us, or worse. The "worse" was never explained, but Tośka and I knew that it was terrible. We learned to be quiet, learned how to contain hunger, and when we had begged enough paper and two pencils, we began to write a novel.

The novel took us far away from Mielec, the Germans, the dangers, and the growing misery. We invented a new fantasy world, a fantasy of adventures and happy endings. We wrote about children like ourselves, of course, who lived what we considered "real lives," as Tośka and I had once lived, long ago it seemed, though it was barely two years since the war had started. They had adventures, perhaps spine-tingling ones, which, however, always turned out well. Our fictional children did not know fear, they helped one another, were never petty or mean. They were sometimes naughty, but never malicious. Time assumed magic dimensions within which we constructed an ideal world where all adventures ended well and where people lived happily ever after. Tośka and I spent untold hours in my corner between the wardrobe and the door, quietly plotting our next adventure. To this day I can still see how Tośka thoughtfully took up her pencil and in her beautiful, precise hand began filling sheets of paper, one after another, with sentences and paragraphs.

In our fantasy world Tośka and I shaped life predictably. There was no war, no one disappeared, no one was beaten to death or changed beyond recognition. In the real world it was different. We saw Mrs. Feiner's daughter again one evening when an autumn chill was already in the air. She and Mrs. Feiner sat on the little porch in front of their cottage where so long ago she had sat with her handsome fiancé. Both women were talking loudly and laughing. Mrs. Feiner's daughter was smoking a cigarette. We opened the gate to the street and looked again. Was this fat woman the beautiful girl we had thought about all spring? Her low-cut dress was much too short, showing her heavy thighs. How was it that she had grown fat when others were getting thinner daily? We could not understand what had happened to the once-beautiful girl whose features were now heavy and coarse.

When she saw us staring at her she began to shout, to curse, her face contorted in violent anger. Tośka and I didn't know what to make of it. We had never seen anyone that angry, or heard such bad language. To be sure, sometimes the crazy woman who lived on the corner of the Small Market carried on like this, but never so violently. Mrs. Feiner's daughter was furious with us—but why? We had done nothing wrong, had done nothing to her. She was obviously blaming us for something, though what this might be we didn't know. We turned and without thinking fled down the street of the burned houses, having so carefully avoided these throughout the year. We fled in terror, as if by running away we could avoid knowing matters we didn't want to know. Yet like the burned houses that were a reminder of death and destruction, Mrs. Feiner's daughter, it turned out, was a reminder of the disintegration war had brought upon us.

Had Cousin Esther been with us that day, she, no doubt, would have explained in plain and unadorned language that Mrs. Feiner's daughter had become a prostitute, and that her brother was pimping for her. That was why Mrs. Feiner had access to flour and potatoes while others did not. But at that point we didn't have the benefit of Cousin Esther's knowledge, which she shared with her friends in whispered conversations and giggles and never with me. Once, I overheard her friend Hava telling her about Hava's Polish maid, in front of whose door men lined up when no one was at home. The girls exchanged knowing glances. I couldn't imagine for what purpose men would wait in front of the maid's room.

I believe now that Tośka and I began to sense (certainly not understand) that there were shameful, unfathomable complexities between men and women. But we weren't ready to acknowledge the disintegration of our fantasy world, which was one of love between men and women. Not yet. I was too young then to appreciate Cousin Esther's ways of dealing with the new reality of our lives. Only much later would I understand that she faced the world squarely, without blinders, recognizing its smuttiness and decay, its horrors and corruption, regardless of the pain this may have caused her. All the same, after the incident with Mrs. Feiner's daughter, Tośka and I no longer talked about her, or even much about love. Matters were no longer as clear as they had been once and words overheard in others' conversations were acquiring new meanings.

In a book recently published about Mielec I read:

In Mielec life was still tranquil. . . . There were no changes in the social and economic conditions or the security of the community. Squads of young Jewish men continued their daily forced labour for German construction companies. The pay was poor but the conditions bearable. Commerce continued, merchants brought goods from Tarnow and Kraków for their Polish and Jewish customers. . . .

Is that how it really was in 1940 and 1941? Or has the long passage of time so dimmed the memory of the author that daily life in that period seems almost pleasant and not one of hardships and fears? Reality can have more than one dimension. Take Uncle Reuven. Since becoming a member of the Judenrat, he was kept busy with community affairs and was no longer to be seen in the store. He was now an important man in town, someone whom others asked for help. His whole appearance seemed to have changed: He walked straighter, he spoke more confidently, and he had lost his earlier sleepy, self-absorbed look. From the cowed, outsider son-in-law in a large family, Uncle Reuven was transformed into a new man with a purpose. Perhaps for him, too, times did not seem altogether bad. Perhaps he, like the author who wrote that life was tranquil, managed to avert his eyes from the daily misery.

As for me, I may not have been unhappy every moment of each day, but I suffered from the ever-present hunger and the shortage of fuel. Since 1940 Jews had had to wear white armbands with the blue Star of David on them whenever they left the house. Not everyone was adept at sewing these armbands and new business ventures started up for their manufacture. Living space continually shrank as Jews were deported to Mielec in ever-growing numbers. Freedom of movement was restricted. No one was allowed to leave town without a permit from the German authorities—which led to an unexpected source of income for us. To obtain a permit, a person had to submit a neatly typed petition to the German authorities. Since Mother knew German and owned a typewriter, she was soon running a business from our little room. Now, from morning until night, people crowded into the little space we had, waiting to have their petitions typed. Strangers were everywhere: on the few chairs, the beds, confiding to one another their problems about out-of-town sick relatives, or talking about business matters that needed attention. During the day there was no longer any room for me or for anyone else in the family; only when night fell could each of us reclaim a bit of space.

Then one day at the onset of winter, when life seemed at its most difficult with the bitter cold, Mother heard of a new school. Jewish youngsters were of course forbidden to go to school after the Germans had come. This new school was, therefore, a clandestine undertaking. It was started by one of the Kraków refugees. She was a Mielec woman who had studied at the university in Kraków and who, when forbidden to continue, had returned home. Attending school was not, however, without its dangers; the teacher might have enemies and someone could denounce her to the Germans, and neighbors might be afraid of being implicated if the Germans were to discover the school. Nonetheless, it was decided I would attend, though caution was called for. I was never to carry books (which in any event I didn't have, never having gone to Polish school), or even copybooks, to and from school. Nor were all of us students to arrive or leave at the same time. If at any time I saw German soldiers or police near the school, Mother warned, I was not to go inside, I was simply to keep on walking.

I was excited, especially since Tośka would also attend. In recent months, whenever I passed the ramshackle small building in the neglected yard where I had studied before the war, I had hoped that by some strange miracle the big padlock would be gone and the one room would once more be filled with eager girls of different ages learning prayers and blessings. I remembered the two young out-of-town teachers in their pretty and fashionable dresses, sleeves covering their elbows and hemlines below the knees, and their patience as they taught us or played games with us. At the end of the year they had arranged an evening performance for the parents, in which I had my glorious moment as a musical chimney sweep.

Cousin Esther, whom I went to inform at once of the new turn in my life, was unable to dampen my pleasure even though she was not impressed. The woman from Kraków is only a university student and not a real teacher, said Cousin Esther. She is giving herself airs because she thinks she is better educated than others. You'll see, Cousin Esther said. School won't be anything like what you imagine. Her mother is just a poor widow who is now putting her daughter to work to get a little money.

For once I didn't argue, mainly because I wasn't sure what people did at universities and how it differed from what we did in school. But Tośka understood Cousin Esther's hostility better than I. Might it not be, she suggested, that Cousin Esther also wants to attend school, but she cannot because her father is a Judenrat official and the school is, after all, illegal?

As I write today I have in front of me a framed photograph of the school's pupils that by some strange twist of fortune survived war and destruction. There are sixteen of us: four boys and twelve girls. We stand next to the house where we studied. I remember only three of my schoolmates' names: Tośka, Tova Trumpeter, and Hava. Tova had bushy brown hair and an easy smile. Her parents lived in the court next to Grandmother Mindel's store. Hava was Cousin Esther's friend. Tośka is in the middle of the photograph like a reigning queen, two boys on each side. Even in this old photograph I can see her golden smile, the smile that made her face glow and her eyes sparkle. Behind her is a girl Tośka and I knew quite well because her baby sister was born with both eyes closed. Two of the boys were from well-to-do families; their parents' stores were on Kolejowa Street. How I wish I knew what happened to each of my schoolmates: what turn their lives took; whom they married, and divorced; which professions they had, or didn't; where they went to live; whether they succeeded or not. But there is nothing to tell. All of my schoolmates except for Tova were killed in Parczew, Włodawa, or Sobibór.

The Ganger sisters in 1916. My mother, Helene, is third from the right.
(Courtesy of the author)

Wedding picture in Halle, Germany, circa 1920. In the third row, to the right of center, are my father (wearing a hat) and, to his left, my mother.
(Courtesy of the Kanner family)

My mother, at far right, with family members
including my sister, Lore, in front. *(Courtesy of Gila Lipper Neta)*

Lore was posing for a photograph.
I jumped up on the bench at the
last second. *(Courtesy of the author)*

From left to right: my dear friend
Toska, a neighbor's child, and me.
(Courtesy of the author)

The local Zionist youth group at an outing in 1937.
Lore is in the first row, at the far left. *(Courtesy of the author)*

My mother and father,
Helene and Yedidia Geminder,
in 1940. They were already
required to wear armbands
bearing the Star of David.
(Courtesy of the author)

In Mielec, in 1940.
From left to right: Lore, Mother,
and my cousin Püppe,
who lived with us at the time.
(Courtesy of the author)

The clandestine school I attended in Mielec, c. 1940–41.
Our teacher is at the center of the last row; at the far right of the last row is
Tova Trumpeter, who survived the war. *(Courtesy of the author)*

THE DEPORTATION FROM MIELEC, ON MARCH 9, 1942.

(Courtesy Felicity Bloch. Photos by Kurt Hippert,
Source Bundes-archiv LB, AR-Z 377/63, BI. 1196)

Some of the town's Jews, with their meager possessions,
on their way to the Large Market, where they were being assembled.

A German soldier watches the Jews gathering.

Young men selected for work
were ordered to deposit their bundles.

Led by a soldier, the men were marched away.

Left behind, an old man sits forlornly on his bundle,
his feet wrapped in rags against the cold.
Most likely, he was shot.

My friend Kuba in Würzburg,
Germany, on October 4, 1945.
Written on the back of this
photo were the words
"To eternal memory, Kuba."
(Courtesy of the author)

A Hanukkah celebration at the displaced persons camp in Cham, Germany,
on December 3, 1945. Sitting at the center in the front is Abie,
who acted as our go-between with the camp authorities.
(Courtesy of the author)

Some of the DPs in front of the Cham Hotel, where they lived. May 1946.
(Courtesy of the author)

My grandmother Mindel's house and store in Mielec,
as it looked in September 1980.
(Courtesy of the author)

The school was not far from our house, on an old street with thatch-roofed houses whose windows were so low that I could look inside without stretching my neck. The houses, being very old, were slowly sinking into the ground, Mother once told me, from which I assumed that they would eventually vanish from view, leaving only the roofs to mark the spot. Our teacher's house, though also very old, had a proper roof. The classroom was the kitchen, since that was the largest room and the only one heated. The teacher's mother cooked while we learned. She came and went throughout the morning, shuffling quietly into the kitchen, moving pots about on the stove, adding an ingredient to one or another. She couldn't have been very old, but with her bent back, her rheumy eyes and missing teeth, she seemed more like the teacher's grandmother.

We sat on benches around two oblong tables. The teacher (whose name to my sorrow I have long forgotten) walked back and forth between the tables, watching us practice writing, asking us questions, or quietly explaining a lesson to us. She never raised her voice, nor were we allowed to speak loudly lest someone passing by outside hear us. I liked her immediately, which is probably the reason why I remember so much about her, even if I have forgotten her name. She was of medium height; her strong and fine-featured face was framed by curly blonde hair. She was not strikingly beautiful, as Mrs. Feiner's daughter had been; rather she had an uncommon dignity, a refined bearing that set her apart from other young women in town. She dressed very simply. Day in, day out, month after month, for all the time I knew her, she wore a turtleneck sweater and a skirt. Though I am sure she must have worn a dress sometimes, my memory has preserved her in a sweater of nondescript color and a somewhat tight skirt.

In the short time that we went to school she taught us many subjects, including the basics of English. We memorized simple

poems that to my unaccustomed ears had deliciously melodic
rhythms, like this one, which I still seem to remember, perhaps
because it tells of the freedom I increasingly longed for:

There was a road ran past our house
Too lovely to explore.
I asked my mother once—she said
That if you followed where it led
It brought you to the milk-man's door.
(That's why I have not travelled more).

Tośka's presence in the kitchen-school cemented our friendship
even more, and Cousin Esther was all but forgotten. Tośka and I
shared the learning and later in the day we shared it again. She
grasped everything quickly and easily. It took me much longer. But
I was not resentful. To the contrary, I enjoyed Tośka's explanations when we relived those precious hours. War, fear, and hunger
vanished from us when we were rehearsing the lessons learned in
the morning. To school Tośka wore a blue schoolgirl's smock from
her Kraków school days; I thought it very chic. I pleaded with
Mother to make a similar outfit for me, and she finally did so as
part of her recycling enterprise when someone sold her the shiny
blue lining of an old coat. During the winter I became very attached to that smock, which had the added advantage of hiding
my increasingly short, threadbare, and patched dresses.

I seldom went home right after school, since I felt uncomfortable around the petitioners and their woes. After I stopped at
Grandmother Mindel's store to let Father know that all was well,
Tośka and I would meet at the Small Market, where she lived.
Unlike our tiny, overstuffed room, her family's two rooms were
spacious and uncluttered, all their belongings having been left
behind in Kraków. Her parents had been lucky to find and keep

these rooms; as a rule four people had no more than one room. Hers was a harmonious family—that is, Tośka, her mother, and her sister were; her father was seldom home. Once Cousin Esther hinted darkly at "another woman," but I covered my ears, not wanting to hear her besmirch my friend's family. I wanted to believe that Tośka's father was trying to do business in town just as mine was.

Mrs. Spyrina was always home when we arrived. She had a melancholy air about her that for some reason made me think of a Spanish dancer with a tragic past, though of course I hadn't ever seen a Spanish dancer. Nor was I quite sure what a tragic past was, except that it seemed to have something to do with unhappy love. Tośka's older sister had inherited their mother's olive skin, but not her temperament. She was perhaps three years older than we, vivacious and amazingly grown-up. The sisters were very fond of each other. Theirs was a much closer relationship than that between me and my sister, who was older by a number of years.

Visiting Tośka meant food. As soon as we arrived, Mrs. Spyrina would cut two slices of black bread and spread them generously with beet jam. After fruit and sugar were no longer available, beet jam made with rutabaga syrup had made its appearance in some households. How beets and rutabaga syrup were turned into jam was, however, rather a mystery, and in our house we had no beet jam. Nor did we ever cut bread slices that thick.

For a short time while we were going to school, a Hebrew teacher, also a Kraków refugee, came into our lives. Father had met him and, no doubt, had taken pity on him, since teachers even more than others were unable to make a living. He came once a week to the Spyrina apartment to give Tośka and me Hebrew lessons. Though we should have been kinder, we thought him outrageously funny. He was a tall, skeletal man dressed in an overcoat several sizes too large. His hat was also oversized, covering his eyebrows and resting on his ears. A dirty brown-gray muffler was wound many times around his neck. It was as if he had lost all his clothes and was now wearing those of a much larger man.

An unvarying ritual accompanied the Hebrew teacher's arrival and departure. He vigorously rubbed his large red hands and, after settling down at the table, pulled a dirty handkerchief from his pocket and noisily blew his nose. A half eggshell, his ashtray, was carefully removed from his other coat pocket, followed by cigarette paper and a tobacco tin. These he placed next to the glass of lime blossom tea that Mrs. Spyrina had brought from the kitchen. After removing his coat, unwinding his muffler, and rolling a cigarette, he was ready for the day's lesson. Five minutes before the hour was up, the same process took place in reverse. The muffler was rewound; into his coat pocket vanished the cigarette paper, tin, and eggshell; he blew his nose, rubbed his still-red hands, and shuffled out the door. One day he was gone and Father told me that during a raid the Germans caught him and sent him to Pustkow.

For a long time thereafter Tośka and I felt guilty for having made fun of him. Everyone has guilt in his or her past, guilt of omission and guilt of commission. Yet the guilt from those days is different, maybe because it is always connected with someone's death, or someone's suffering and misfortune. Innocent acts, so natural to children, are unreasonably merged with questions of life and death. To this day I feel guilty for ridiculing the destitute and unfortunate man.

SEPTEMBER 1980

Stanisław, the driver, picks me up early in the morning at the Hotel Francuski in Kraków for the drive to Mielec. I am tense, feeling almost the same kind of anxious tension I used to feel before taking a test. And indeed, the visit to Mielec is meant to be, aside from everything else, an examination of sorts, a test of my memory. How accurate is my memory of the town, and are the places I remember in fact where I think they are? What if I've gotten it all wrong and nothing is as I remember it to be?

We arrive in Mielec in a few hours, and as we enter the town I have my first jolt: The market square, although still very much recognizable as the Large Market, is no longer a barren cobblestone expanse. It has been transformed into a kind of park with trees and shrubs, kiosks and bus stops. The road that dissected the market diagonally is now properly paved. The same prewar houses ring the square, but in some of them the passages that led to streets behind the market are now closed up.

We drive through the market and park the car on Kolejowa Street, now called Mickiewicza Street after the famous Polish poet. I suddenly realize that I have entered a miniaturized world. Houses that once were large are now small; places once at distances that took time to cover are now close by. The once-elegant house on the corner of Kolejowa and Sandomierska is now quite ordinary, and the bakery, where I brought the cholent Friday afternoons, is only a few steps from Grandmother Mindel's house. Sandomierska 15 has changed into a rather small house, and it is no longer painted a gloomy gray but a slightly more cheerful rust color. The little court where we played hopscotch, having grown even smaller, is still at the side of the house, and so is the Trumpeters' store at the end of it. The staircase from the court to the second-story apartment above the store is still there, but the new owners have replaced the wooden steps with stone. Gone, at the entrance, is the trapdoor to the cellar, where on market days Grandmother Mindel kept the ill-fated chickens with their legs tied together. The passage leading from the court to the Large Market square, which always reeked because boys and men alike urinated in its dark recesses, is closed off. Perhaps there are now public toilets in Mielec.

I walk down Sandomierska toward the Small Market. Gone is

the spacious Friedman house, the rebbe's ramshackle place, and the Talmud Torah next to it where the boys studied. A large food store stands where once there had been the fine stone synagogue, erected in 1902, with its two imposing towers. Fresh produce is sold at the Small Market, where the Geminder family of Hayim-the-Small once had their homes, but the market square is even smaller than it was in the past. I go directly to the house of Mime Rivke of the Geminder family, a sickly woman who had a great many unmarried daughters. Directly across from that building is the house where Tośka and her family had their two rooms. I see something I have not noticed before: Where the mezuzah had been on the wooden doorpost there remains only the imprint of its shape, a Jewish ghost that will be banished, never to reappear when the house is torn down. Poland is full of such ghosts, crying silently in hidden crevices, turning up in half-exposed Hebrew inscriptions on houses and in unexpected places, as I discover on this journey. I hear the ghosts' whispers, I see the gaping emptiness of a mezuzah's impression on a doorpost. Stanisław, the driver, doesn't understand when I stop to listen, or why I look at doorposts.

Even if our Hebrew lessons were short-lived, and our careers as students did not last much longer, in the little time left to us Tośka's horizons and mine were becoming larger. We were not stagnating. And sometime during the winter we made a new friend. He was a young man, a refugee from Kraków who, like our teacher, had been a student and who lived in a rented room across the street from us. He was very pale and thin and had the most extraordinarily pink palms. Leaning on his windowsill, he had once called out a greeting to me as I was passing his house. He made lighters, he said, now that matches were impossible to find. (To this day I wonder what those lighters were like.) After that, whenever I saw his open window, I stopped to ask about the lighters and we talked for a few minutes. He must have been lonely, without either family or friends in Mielec. Mother had nothing against him, she told me, but he was unfortunately a very sick young man. He had consumption—a terrible and very contagious disease—so I was to keep my distance and not touch him.

In time Tośka and I discovered that even if he had not brought many possessions with him to Mielec, he did have quite a few books that he not only was very happy to lend us, but also looked forward to discussing after we had read them. This was how I made my first acquaintance with Sherlock Holmes and Tom Sawyer. Suddenly we discovered new and unknown worlds, strange places we had never heard of, strange ways of telling stories. We delighted in the tricks Tom played on poor Aunt Polly and we approved her loving him in spite of them. Mark Twain's fictional small-town world was as circumscribed as our real one, but there were exits from that one, whereas ours had none. Following Tom on his raft downriver to the island, we had a new vision of freedom, of the delights of nature accessible in the strange, great country of America and its open spaces. Tom's world and ours were vastly different and we had to ask many questions about riverboats and Indians, about the puzzle of trials and justice, about fear and courage. Our new friend also lent us books by Karl May, wonderful adventure stories about American Indians and the West, even about China, a land so far away neither Tośka nor I could fathom the distance. We had to beg our friend to explain the mysteries of time and space.

Sometimes Tośka and our friend talked about places closer to home. Both from Kraków, they never tired of extolling the wonders of the Wawel, the castle of the Polish kings, with its endless rooms, its paintings, and its furnishings. Tapestries hung everywhere; according to Tośka, young maidens, companions to the queens, embroidered them year in and year out. They stitched wonderful pictures of meadows and trees, and men, women, and children, while waiting for their beloved knights to return from distant journeys. The knights went by ship, sailing on the broad Vistula to lands few had ever seen. I tried to picture the wonders the two described in such detail. But I had never been to Kraków and our Wisłoka River was not very broad. One day, years hence, I too would see the Wawel, but by then my heart would ache over being alive while my friend was dead. I seemed to recall, however, in the course of these conversations, that once even Mielec had a castle. A long time ago, when of an afternoon the women still told stories in Grandmother Mindel's kitchen, one had described a castle on the Wisłoka. She swore that as a child her brothers showed her its proud walls and gates and ruined towers. She remembered from long ago a strange story about a Jewish girl who fell in love with a Polish knight. But the women scoffed at her—none remembered a castle nearby. And how could a Jewish girl be in love with a Polish man? they wanted to know. Yet Tośka and our new friend thought it quite possible.

These images are all incomplete, as if refracted in a shattered mirror. Some are larger, some are smaller, but something is missing in each broken fragment. Certain qualities have gone astray— the way a person smiled, moved, talked; qualities that reveal something about a person's inner nature. We had no time to really get to know each other. For brief moments, when Tośka and I walked together, our paths crossed those of the teacher, our friend across the way, or of Mrs. Feiner and her daughter, until, scattered in the whirlwind of death and destruction, each one disappeared.

I had a friend. Her name was Tośka. She died in Bełżec.

CHAPTER FIVE

SOUP KITCHENS AND TAPESTRIES

Kum tsu mir tsurik mayn Hankele	*Return to me my Hankele*
Kum tsu mir tsurik mayn kroyn	*Return to me my crown*
Kum tsu mir tsurik mayn Hankele	*Won't you come back to me my Hankele*
Vayl ikh bin tsu dir gevoynt.	*For I'll not make it on my own.*
Treblinke dort.	*Treblinka there.*
Far yedn Yid a guter ort.	*For every Jew there's tender care.*
Ver's kumt ahin farblaybt	*All who come there remain*
shoyn dort	*Remain eternally.*
Farblaybt oyf eybig.	*Whoever comes there,*
Ver's kumt ahin fun brider,	*brother, sister, father, mother*
shvester, tate, mamen	
Den tut men zey oykhet glaykh	*Is poisoned at once*
farsamen	
Un dos iz zeyer sof.	*And that is their end.*
Fun di vagonen tut men aropyogn	*Rushed from the train without respite*
In toyten lager arayn	*Into the death camp to their fate*
A bod tut men zey opzogen	*A bath, they're told, will make you fit*
S'hert zikh oys a groys geveyn	*Their cries are heard beyond the gate.*
Treblinke dort. . . .	*Treblinka there. . . .*

From a song sung by many Jews in Kraków in the summer of 1945

When my daughter was fourteen and then fifteen years old, she and I lost our connection to each other, as if one day I no longer knew how to talk to her. Indeed, I hardly seemed to recognize her. Somewhere in those grubby jeans, that oversized jacket, hidden behind untidy hair and hostile eyes, was my sweet and gentle daughter, but I didn't know how to find her. At the time I believed this loss of connection to be mostly her fault— teenage trials, I said, a condition that was in my opinion exacerbated by the scandalous conduct of her father, the man I had married. Only much later, after the hurt of the disconnection had healed, did I begin to understand that the kind of person I was at a similar age had contributed to my daughter's being how she was at age fifteen. But the problem that I did not understand at the time is more complex. When I was her age I was a "hidden child," as it is now the fashion to say. Not having experienced either an emotional or a social development in those years, nor having, for that matter, developed intellectually, I call that time a "black hole." I think of it as a darkness in which there was only fear, and not much else one associates with living. The ages of fourteen and fifteen eluded me as part of growing up. With no experience to draw on, I didn't know how to guide my daughter during those difficult years. Oddly, she seems to have sensed that.

Who I was at war's end in 1945 was not at all clear to me. Several documents from 1945 reveal the confusion. They attest to my health, attendance in school, permission to travel, and identity. They are commonplace, everyday documents, except that each has slightly different information: The date of birth is either 1927, 1929, or 1930; the place of birth is different in each case, and so is my name. Are the differences due to bureaucratic error, or did I supply contradictory information? On some papers I was in

Theresienstadt, on others no place is stated. That I was hidden does not appear anywhere, that category of surviving did not exist as yet. In 1945 one had to have been somewhere with a recognizable name. Bureaucrats who either filled out or scrutinized documents would not have been able to relate only to a chicken coop. At the age of fifteen I, therefore, had neither a definite name, age, nor place of birth, and was even unable to show clearly how I had managed to stay alive.

Obvious to me in my bewildered state in Kraków in the summer of 1945 was only that the Germans were defeated, the Russians had come, and I was alive. But memory is not chronological. Events and impressions are not neatly filed away in some kind of order; something is remembered and then something similar or very different comes to mind. Alas, I cannot fit my account of hiding in a chicken coop and then emerging alive into a tidy, logically arranged sequence in order to explain how it was that I came to be in Kraków.

JUNE 1998

I am having coffee with Alice, who was born in Poland, and Sheila, an American friend, in the elegantly renovated faculty club at the Hebrew University's Mount Scopus campus. The view of Jerusalem from Beit Maiersdorf is spectacular. Below is the walled Old City—the golden cupola of the Dome of the Rock, the slim church spires, and the domed or flat roofs of its many buildings. Beyond is West Jerusalem, its skyline ever changing as new high-rises make their appearance, although the King David Hotel and the YMCA tower behind it are still major landmarks from our vantage point on the faculty club terrace. On the horizon, in the distance, is the minaret of Samuel's Tomb, where the grand old man who anointed King David is presumably buried. A shepherd has brought his flock of sheep to graze on the mountainside behind the campus. We can hear the delicate tinkling of the bells he has tied around his donkey's neck.

I tell my friends that I survived the war hidden in a chicken coop by a kindhearted Polish family. Alice is impressed. She looks at me admiringly, as if I had accomplished an extraordinary feat. I am not used to being admired for surviving in a chicken coop and I bask in this quite unexpected moment of glory. After all, I cannot lay claim to being descended from a long line of rabbis and, except for my great-grandmother Blime, who wore a turban with strands of pearls and was married to three husbands, there is precious little I can boast of in my past. Sheila, however, is not impressed. She wants to know what I did in the chicken coop for nearly two years. An odd question, which I don't know how to answer—how can one be doing something in a chicken coop?

I was alone in that place, I want to tell her. Alone! Day after day. Night after night. And the nights were long, unending, the days short and gray; and in winter night merged into day, day into night. Always black or gray. How many days and nights, weeks, months? Do you think I counted them? I want to ask Sheila. Would it have made a difference? I knew only the seasons—the long season of cold and night, the short season of warmth and light. I was alone and afraid. What are the words for the nameless terrors of long black nights? No, for this kind of aloneness there are no words. In this kind of aloneness there is no *doing.* It is timeless, it lasts forever.

I say none of this to Sheila. Alice smiles knowingly. She understands where others don't, or perhaps can't. It occurs to me that Sheila, in fact most people, can have no idea what a Polish chicken coop was like. Their familiarity with chicken coops probably comes only from television, which shows the poor chickens in cages high above the ground—hardly a hiding place. I realize that I must try to explain to Sheila what my Polish chicken coop was like.

In the yard there were four or five flimsy wooden shacks, each with a padlocked door, standing in a row where the tenants of the apartment house kept egg-laying hens. The Orlowskys had a shack that measured perhaps two by four meters where they kept chickens and rabbits. Rabbits are placid animals; they eat, wriggle their noses, and rustle whatever is rustleable in their cages. But chickens are easily aroused; they are nervous and cackle noisily when disturbed. Hens lay eggs starting in early spring and continue through late fall, even after the weather has turned cold. During the egg-laying months, it was believed, they had to be allowed to scratch in the dirt, to supplement their diet with pebbles and grasses. However, care had to be taken to confine those hens that were about to lay an egg to the coop. Otherwise the hen might lay the egg in the yard where neighbors could steal it. I ask Sheila if she has ever seen a chicken lay an egg, and of course she hasn't. They labor at it, I tell her, straining fearfully as if they were constipated, until at last the egg pops out. Hard to believe, I know, that a chicken can look relieved.

Therefore, I explain to Sheila, who is increasingly impatient with this digression into the habits of chickens, there was constant traffic in and out of the shack, for as soon as the egg was laid someone would come to let the chicken out. And while this made possible the conveying of messages, it also made it necessary to be especially careful. I had to remain well hidden so that the neighbors who were similarly taking care of their chickens would neither see nor hear me.

The chicken routine was different during the winter months. When it snowed, the birds were not let out, since they were not able to scratch in the yard. During the cold winter months the door to the shack was not often open. Days were short and nights were long; gloomy twilight or complete darkness seemed to last forever. Alice would like to hear more, but Sheila is not interested in these detailed descriptions. Why doesn't she ask me about the smell? I wonder. Does she think rabbits and chickens come perfumed? Why isn't she curious what I smelled like, living as it were in a compost heap? But then, why should she ask? After all, Sheila has never smelled the stink of a chicken coop. We drink our coffee and turn to admire Jerusalem glowing golden in the setting sun.

To me, Kraków in the summer of 1945 was all incongruities, fragmented pieces of experience none of which fitted with any other; it was a summer of many things told and much left unsaid. New impressions at every turn were crowded into a short span of about two months. Although I had no one to share them with, to explain them to me, to help me understand, I absorbed the incongruities, made them mine, stored them away without order and without trying to make sense of them.

I avoided people that summer and wanted to be alone. Yet being alone was precisely the reason I was unhappy. I avoided the noisy women who crowded the small apartment where I lived, and then envied them their conviviality. My daily task was to fetch soup from the soup kitchen; it gave me ample opportunity to wander about alone. Each day I tried to take a different route to the soup kitchen. Sometimes I went by way of the Small Market square in back of St. Mary's church. The market was crowded and noisy, with brisk trading in clothes and food. A line of women stood off to the side. Over their outstretched arms they had draped coats, shirts, and dresses, and in front of each woman stood a basket into which she put the food she had received in payment for a piece of clothing. Sharp-eyed peasant women with baskets over their arms walked slowly up and down, fingering a dress here, inspecting a pair of shoes there. The line of women stood motionless like living clothes racks, staring stonily ahead of them.

Sometimes I avoided the Small Market and instead cut through Mariacki Square to the Main Market square and the Sukiennica, the Cloth Hall, where I sat down under its graceful arcades. Across from it was St. Mary's, of impressive height and proportions, its entrance flanked by two towers—one taller than the other—and as busy as can be. Barefoot peasant women in long skirts and colorful shawls streamed in and out of the imposing church. Nuns and monks came and went, and groups of children vanished within the edifice as if swallowed up, never to be seen again. Russian soldiers stopped in the middle of the square to stare up at the great height of the church, and some went to the entrance to peek inside. From the vantage point of the Cloth Hall I too was awed by the beauty of St. Mary's, and I enjoyed the movement of the colorful crowd. Before the war, someone told me, a bugle call was sounded every hour on the hour from the taller of the two towers. But that summer the bugler was not in evidence.

I often went inside, mingling with the peasant women, crossing myself at the entrance with consecrated water, then kneeling as I said an Our Father. I liked being in the splendid edifice, feasting my eyes on the rich sculpture, the paintings, and the colorful stained-glass windows. Here were scenes not only from the lives of Jesus and the saints, but also from Genesis, the first book of the Bible, familiar to me from another life. I liked being among these devout Christians, being taken as one of them. I wasn't pretending; I felt this is where I truly belonged. I saw myself as one of these Polish people, one of these religious believers, and this beautiful church was mine as much as theirs.

It rarely rained that summer in Kraków. The days were unbelievably bright, filled with the kind of golden sunshine I had so

missed during my chicken coop years. The subdued light of the
church and the sun's warm rays on my skin, face, and hair were
indescribable pleasures. I always left St. Mary's satisfied and went
back to the Cloth Hall, from where I again watched the people in
the Main Market and admired the splendid buildings that surrounded it. Most of the buildings were dilapidated, even to my
untrained eye, and in a state of disrepair. I could not help but
think of Tośka, who had been the one to tell me of Kraków's
splendors, the beauty of its buildings, the majesty of its squares.
But of course I could not grasp what I was seeing. Many years
later I would learn that the Main Market was one of the finest
remaining examples of Renaissance squares and its buildings
were representative of Renaissance architecture. There were not
only the elegant tall windows of many houses but also the splendidly decorated parapets. Each day I sat and stared and let the sun
warm my discolored, frostbitten toes in the oversized sandals,
until it was time for my Polish Catholic half to rejoin the Jewish
half at the soup kitchen.

The great day for most Jews, when living could be ever so cautiously resumed, was when the gates of the camps were flung
open, when the Germans melted into the countryside, and when
some of us crawled out of our hiding places. I hadn't thought
of, hadn't dared to imagine, such a day. Indeed, I had guarded
against all hope, thinking rather of what I must do if I were discovered hiding. I would certainly not want to endanger the good
people who had saved me, and above all I would not grovel for my
life. Let them shoot me, let them beat me to death—I hoped that I
would have the strength and courage not to beg for mercy.

In July 1944 I began to receive, at chicken-feeding or egg-
checking time, whispered reports that the Russians were advanc-

ing and the Germans were retreating; then that the Russians were retreating and the Germans were advancing, or American planes were seen over Mielec, or the Germans were leaving with the machines from the aircraft factory. At night there were house searches. The Germans were increasingly nervous and afraid of partisans, I was told, and I said to myself that at the first sign of danger I would leave the chicken coop and run.

Fortunately, before long the Russian offensive began. I heard shooting once distant now near, and it created within me a strange and unknown feeling that I couldn't remember having before, a feeling—no, the conscious thought—of hope that I might after all remain alive. That I might actually live to see the day when every last German, including Rudi Zimmermann, would be dead and I alive and free to walk about again unafraid. I don't know how Mielec was liberated. I remained in my chicken coop that day, for even if the Germans had left and the Russians were on their way, the former might return and the latter not advance as quickly. Besides, one had no way of knowing what defeated Germans were capable of doing. No one had any illusions about German brutality.

I don't remember what kind of day August 6, 1944, was. Did it rain? Was it sunny? Overcast? Cool, hot? All I remember about that day is that once it was certain that the front had moved beyond Mielec, I walked out of the shack in the evening twilight, under a windswept sky of many colors. My time of aloneness had lasted one year and ten months. But this occurred to me only much later, after I had relearned how to take stock of time. What I remember of that evening were the tired-looking Russian soldiers who sat in the Orlowsky kitchen drinking vodka, relaxing, before having to move on. Was I happy to see them? Perhaps I was too numb to have such an unused, almost forgotten feeling. Among them were soldiers I took to be Tatars, but was later told were Kalmuks. It was my first encounter with non-Europeans.

In the days that followed, more Russian soldiers came, including women soldiers. No slouchers they: Standing ramrod straight at intersections, they rapidly twirled two little flags held in either hand—right, left, right, or straight ahead—directing the heavy truck traffic moving westward. Other women soldiers belonged to laundry details; one of these moved large tubs and scrubbing boards into the spare room of the Orlowskys' apartment and heated water on improvised stoves in the yard. At night the soldiers gave concerts for the Mielec population, and I thought I had never heard a more wonderful song than "Kalinka" or seen more accomplished dancing than in the "Kozak." I was sure that those spirited women singers were none other than our laundry soldiers who during the day washed uniforms in people's spare rooms. Somehow they all looked alike: short and stout with blonde hair and blue eyes, their uniform blouses belted so tight it seemed to cut off their breath. I sat in the audience, wonderfully unafraid as if having shed a sickening burden, no longer fearing anyone or anything. I felt as Polish and (presumably) as free as everyone else in that audience.

Although Mielec may have been liberated, the war was far from over. Battles continued in the vicinity and it was not until five months later, in mid-January 1945, that the brutal German governor, Hans Frank, and the rest of the Germans left Kraków. Poles, to be sure, suffered under the German occupation, but there were also those whose conscience regarding their erstwhile Jewish neighbors was not very clean. Prudently, the Orlowskys and I decided not to mention my being Jewish. And so it was that I became an orphaned relative, surnamed Orlowsky, charitably taken in by the family. I was not apprehensive that Polish people who had known me five or six years before would recognize me. In 1944 I was a fourteen-year-old with long braids who spoke fluent, unaccented Polish. Now, in 1944, my new identity was perhaps not yet entirely comfortable. But as the months wore on, being a Polish Catholic orphan felt increasingly natural, like a well-worn pair of shoes gradually molded to one's feet. I was a Polish girl even after the Orlowskys left Mielec, taking me along to Poznań, where they had lived before the war.

I evolved almost naturally into a Polish Catholic orphan—in part because time was passing, day after day, week after week while I waited, and no one came looking for me. I had neither word from nor news of my family. We had, of course, little accurate information about the progress of the war, about which areas were still occupied and which liberated, or about all of what had really happened to Jews in the last two years. There was the floating soap that no one bought, because people believed that it was made with human fat, and we knew, of course, about Majdanek, which had been liberated in 1944 by the Russian army.

Increasingly I was convinced that when I left Dębica I had abandoned my family to certain death, saving only myself. Thus, make-believe gradually turned into belief and I thought that I was indeed an orphan, that everyone—parents, sister, uncles, aunts, cousins—was killed. Of all my family, I thought, I was the only one alive. More than that, I eventually was convinced that I was the only Jew left alive. I neither heard of nor saw another Jew in Mielec or later in Poznań (only recently was I told of several Jews in Mielec at the time who, like myself, had been hidden). If I was an orphan and the only remaining Jew, what difference did it make if I were a Jewish or a Catholic orphan? I reasoned. If I could not admit now that I was Jewish, why pretend that not being Jewish was only temporary? How could I be sure that being Jewish would be less dangerous later? I could become a new person, I said to myself as the months after liberation lengthened into nearly one year. I could become a person unselfishly dedicated to helping others, to living for others, a person living only to end wars, killing, and bloodshed. I would not be a burden to the good people who saved me from certain death. I would become a nun, live in a convent among like-minded women. Whatever the reason for choosing to be a nun—and I suspect guilt haunted me over abandoning my family—having found a goal in life was comforting and even seemed to give meaning to being the last Jew alive. Exactly how to go about becoming a nun did not matter at the time, as long as there was a plan.

But then one day when summer was just beginning to assert itself, Sister arrived at the Orlowskys' in Poznań. My carefully constructed new self, having been quite satisfactory for nearly a year, was suddenly in shambles. Suddenly I was no longer an orphan, for Mother too was alive. How Sister had found me in these still-uncertain times, neither she nor I remember, although she may have told me then or later. But there was no time to reflect, no time to feel sorrow for having to part from the good people who had saved my life. Taking my hastily packed bundle of clothing, I left with Sister for the train station.

The train sped through the night toward Kraków, Poznań already far behind. Sometimes I saw the sparks fly from the locomotive, sometimes I heard the mournful whistle. The train was crowded, as were all trains in Poland in spring and summer of 1945. Everyone seemed to be going somewhere: leaving the camps and places the Germans had dragged people off to, and making their way home; searching for relatives, hoping to find them alive; trying to leave this land drenched in blood and the homes where strangers had come to live.

Sister and I were wedged tightly between two women from the countryside. At least we didn't have to travel in a cattle car. Trains still frightened me, bringing back scenes I didn't want to remember.

Sister was as beautiful as ever and I loved her because she was my sister, but she was a stranger to me, as I probably was to her. Only a few hours before, I was a Polish Catholic on my way to becoming a nun someday. Only a few hours before, I thought I was the last Jew, a secret Jew. Now there were two of us. Sister said Mother was also alive. She was in Kraków. So there were three of us. What would Mother be like? Would she be a stranger like Sister? The train sped through the dark night. Far behind were the Orlowskys, the familiar house, the streets, the school I had been going to, and where only this morning my classmates and I had taken the teacher's dictation:

Dyktando   8 VI 45

Bogaty młynarz zbudował sobie śliczny dom. Murarze wnieśli murowane ściany, blacharz pokrył blachą dach. . . .

(A rich miller built himself a beautiful house. Masons erected brick walls, the tinsmith covered the roof with sheeting. . . .)

Early morning, the sun is just rising. I stand in the apartment to which Sister has brought me. I am wearing a shapeless sort of pink-beet-red dress. My hair is windblown, my braids having gotten untidy during the long train ride. Mother and I look at each other. We don't fall into each other's arms weeping ecstatically over being reunited, as such scenes have often been portrayed in movies. We both stand there in the early morning sun and look: two strangers, the same and not the same, mother and daughter. Each has thought and feared the other dead, yet for more than two years Mother has remained alive by luck and her wits, and I am alive because good people took pity on me and I learned how to pretend not to exist. I was alone, I had abandoned myself; indeed, it was I who also had abandoned everyone to save myself. Mother is not to blame, nor am I, that I don't know what to say to her and she doesn't know what to say to me. In the small space of the kitchen there is an abyss between myself and my mother, an abyss neither one of us is able to cross. Many years later I will be a mother and my daughter will be, as I was then, fifteen years old, and we too will not know what to say to each other, even if fears about living or dying are no longer the reason. But just as I and Mother eventually will find a way of managing with our pain, so my daughter and I too will learn to deal with a sorrow I unknowingly and unintentionally had bequeathed to her.

Kraków was beautiful, strange, a world unknown, where nothing matched, nothing made sense, everything was contradictory. I lived, as it were, in three spheres, and in each I was both the same and not the same, moving with ease from the role of the Polish Catholic girl praying in St. Mary's church to that of the Jewish girl waiting for the soup kitchen to open and, more reluctantly, to the role of daughter and sister.

The Jewish soup kitchen on Długa Street, or Long Street, was quite a distance from the Main Market, though I did not mind the long walk up Sławkowska Street past ancient Holy Mark's church to the other side of the Planty gardens. A lively scene invariably greeted me at the soup kitchen, where people tended to congregate well before the place opened. They were from everywhere, it seemed: from all parts of Poland, from Hungary, Czechoslovakia, Ukraine; there were already even some returnees from beyond the Urals (the so-called Asiatics), dispatched to those inhospitable regions by the Soviet government years earlier. Faces changed each day; some people departed, new ones arrived. Only very few like myself stood day after day in the soup line. We greeted each other like old acquaintances.

There were always fewer women than men (actually boys, puny and stunted, who had not grown up the way teenagers normally do). Everyone wore ill-fitting clothes, picked up here and there ("organized," we called it), too short or too long, patched and never very clean. Some of the boys were boisterous and loud, others were withdrawn, with a faraway look in their eyes as if still seeing scenes for which there were as yet no words. Despite impatience and grumbling—the soup kitchen always opened late, although not having watches we could not tell the time—the crowd was cheerful. They joked, told long stories, and sang songs. "Treblinka" was my favorite, and I wrote down the words on scraps of paper.

If I were to reconstruct a typical soup kitchen conversation, it might go something like this:

"Waiting, waiting, always waiting," one person would grumble. "Wasting our precious days."

And another would counter, "Why complain, friend? A beautiful day, the sun is shining, we're free, the Germans are dead, what more do you want?"

Some were bitter. "Waiting for a ladle of soup like beggars. What kind of a life is this? The dreams we had about the end of war. Just look at us now, again lining up for a bite to eat."

And then someone down the line would begin to sing:

Return to me my Hankele
Return to me my crown.
Won't you come back to me my Hankele
For I'll not make it on my own.
  Treblinka there
  For every Jew there's tender care. . . .

Sometimes groups of Russian soldiers passed by in their clean uniforms, their faces round and ruddy. With that satisfied look of people who have just eaten a large meal, they curiously eyed the rowdy soup line, laughed (I always thought derisively), and walked on. But finally the soup would arrive, or be cooked at last, the half doors would be opened, and we would present our large and small pots to the women who filled them with the brownish or greenish liquid. Each day the women complained about my large pot, filling it nonetheless, but warning that tomorrow I would get only one portion.

Despite the mornings spent among the more sedate Polish churchgoers on the Main Market, I did not feel uncomfortable in this lively Yiddish-speaking crowd. Even if some complained, others had an infectious sense of humor that I recognized from another life and that apparently led me to write a poem (at least, I think it is mine). It is dated July 1945. A rough translation from the Polish reads as follows:

The Committee on Long Street
has vast numbers of departments
where they search
for people from many lands.
Charitably they dole out
half a liter of pea soup, beets, and jam,
sometimes even a slice of bread.
Meanwhile frying in the kitchen
is meat for the hundred secretaries
who, working in the sweat of their brow,
never feel low
eating sausage for breakfast—
no wonder
they gain ten kilos each week.

Not great poetry, to be sure, either in Polish or in English. Still, I wonder why I chose poetry and not prose to express my dismay about corrupt humanity. Perhaps I was thinking of Toška and the beautiful poems only she knew how to write.

I would carry my full pot of soup back to the apartment where Mother waited to "stretch" it with either carrots or potatoes that two of the women we lived with had managed to trade on the Small Market. After all, my pot of soup was hardly enough to feed seven of us. Everyone being busy with various chores, however, I was the only one fit for waiting long hours in the soup line. Food was not plentiful in Kraków that summer, and aside from the soup kitchen food, other delicacies, like cheese or an occasional egg, were obtained by barter, provided of course one had something to exchange that the peasant women wanted. These were very serious and time-consuming business transactions.

The women in the apartment (I don't know whose apartment it was, Celina's or Regina's), although a strangely assorted lot, had common bonds in which I was not included. Mother, Sister, Regina, and Mania were close to one another, having been together in the Płaszów concentration camp and, there, having managed to get on Oskar Schindler's list. They ended up in Brünlitz, from where they returned to Kraków, Regina's home. Celina and her mother were Regina's friends who had survived on false papers. In their well-fitting, even if in places threadbare, dresses, they seemed more settled, leading more orderly lives than the others, perhaps because they, although they lived under constant danger of detection, had been less dislocated. I remember Celina's mother as a garrulous elderly lady, while Celina with her stunning tan and her peroxide-blonde hair seemed a being from another world. Mania, who was closest to me in age, was the most cheerful and friendly, but Regina, with her sparkling black eyes and energetic movements, was the undisputed leader and manager, though just what it was that she managed I cannot remember.

Each day, Regina brought news or had some eagerly awaited piece of information, and she was an altogether commanding presence among these returnees from the very brink of death. She had many friends, old friends from before the war, new ones she made on her daily rounds; they came and went, crowding the small apartment, talking, forever talking about this or that person thought to be alive, seen last by someone on a forced march, in a train station, or now on the committee list of people known to be alive that was posted each day. They talked about leaving Poland, how to leave Russian-occupied Poland, how to reach the American zone, how to leave for Palestine; they were forever planning, and then just sitting there safe and comfortable among friends.

Mother moved silently among these talkative men and women. She was part of them, yet strangely remote. She was so thin, almost skeletal. She stood at the stove in a faded, oversized dress, cooking, peering myopically (she badly needed glasses) into small and large pots, adding whatever was lacking, her thin face serious and her dull brown hair drawn back into a sparse knot. In a photograph taken shortly after we left Kraków, Mother's large eyes are still frightened in an emaciated face full of pain and sorrow. It is the face I remember from when we first saw each other after Sister and I returned from Poznań.

Not then in Kraków, nor later, did Mother talk about Father, even though once she settled down to a new life, with a new husband in a new country, she talked frequently and at length about the past. But in Kraków it was Sister who told me the bare outline of how Father, the sweet singer of songs no one else knew, was killed.

After everyone was deported from the Dębica ghetto in October 1942, two hundred people, the great majority of them men, were allowed to remain in what was now a labor camp. As I said earlier, among those on the list were Mother and Uncle Reuven. Neither Aunt Feige nor Cousin Esther, nor Father and Sister, neither Uncle Reuven's younger sister, Hanka, were on the list. As far as the German machine of death was concerned, all had been on the train to Auschwitz, and had ceased to exist. Uncle Reuven had been unable to save anyone else. Father and the others realized then, as I had earlier, that they could not hide indefinitely. Each day the Germans searched houses and cellars and sought out hastily erected walls concealing Jews. Only one choice remained: They had to leave, though not all at once. They would make their way to Cyranka-Berdechow, the labor camp, established in the forest near Mielec after the Radomyśl deportation earlier in summer, where Cousin Malka already was. Perhaps this had been Uncle Reuven's plan. He might still have had connections, ways of communicating with people who mattered and were influential. Sister and Uncle Reuven's younger sister, Hanka, left first. They walked at night and hid in the daytime, planning to arrive at the camp at daybreak, when they would join the work detail leaving the camp. Either the guards did not notice or, what is more likely, they were bribed in some way by Uncle Reuven through Malka. The two girls worked all day together with the road construction detail, returning to the camp with the others in the evening.

Father, Aunt Feige, and Cousin Esther left Dębica a few days later. For the three of them, two no longer young, walking the more than twenty miles to the camp in cold weather and perhaps snow or rain must have been exhausting. They may not have had enough food to sustain them; it may have taken longer than they thought. Nonetheless, having managed somehow to get inside the camp while nearly everyone was at work outside, they decided to rest in one of the barracks. And that is where the German guards found them. They took them outside and shot all three.

Thereafter, whenever I thought of my father, only his last moments of life came to mind. I imagined him tired, hungry, and cold, with laughing guards in German uniforms pointing guns at him as he was made to dig his grave, each shovel of dirt bringing

him closer to death. He dug, knowing that when the hole was sufficiently large and deep his life would end. How long did it take
him to dig his grave? How long did he live before the shot rang out
and he fell into the grave?

But this is not how it happened. I learned recently that in this
camp were three brothers (or was it only one?), named Kaplan,
who were Gestapo informers. They were free to come and go as
they pleased, using their freedom not only to betray Jews sheltered by Poles in the vicinity of Mielec, but also to give away anyone who had come into the camp illegally. I don't know if they did
it to ingratiate themselves with the Germans, hoping thereby to
save their own skins. Was it malice, or personal grudges against
people from Mielec they had known? Whatever the reason, it was
a Kaplan who informed the Germans about the three tired fugitives in the barracks. Father, Aunt Feige, and Cousin Esther were
apparently shot in the camp but not made to dig their graves. The
bodies of the three were left to lie where they had fallen for all to
see when they returned from their day of hard labor. Later they
were buried in the forest surrounding the camp. To this day somewhere in a forest near Mielec in an unmarked grave are their
remains, as are the bones of many other victims of the Kaplans
and the Germans.

Each day in Kraków, after our midday meal, Mother put on a
clean though equally ill-fitting dress and set off for the committee
to read those endless lists of people still alive that kept appearing.
Each evening she returned with her face lined more deeply with
grief, her eyes more hopeless. Never in all those weeks did she find
a familiar name of a relative or friend.

Mania and Sister went daily to the Small Market to engage in
some serious trading and Celina went to her office job. Celina's

mother was left in charge of the apartment. She sat in the one comfortable chair dreaming, I imagined, of the past when she was well off; when she had Persian carpets and a Persian lamb coat; when she still had a husband; and when perhaps, not unlike our Mrs. Friedman in Mielec, she went on her round of visits in the afternoon. I spent my afternoons discovering Kraków.

Learning this beautiful city as if reading portions of a book seems to have been born as much from a desire to taste my new freedom as it was from (I thought then) a determination to lead my Polish life. Out there, in the beautiful Planty gardens, in the little squares and old churches, among the awe-inspiring build-ings of Jagiełłonian University and its secluded courtyards, I felt strangely at home. But I had no way of knowing then, no experi-ence to guide me and no mentor to explain, that what I was really responding to in this city was the history and traditions it pre-served. Kraków was my first encounter with history as well as with art and beauty. And in Kraków I sensed a life, a world beyond Poland, and beyond the dilemma of being Jewish and having remained alive. Perhaps it was then that a small seed was planted, one that would remain dormant for many years but that eventu-ally pointed the way toward loving antiquity (*hao gu,* as the Chi-nese call it) and cherishing history.

In Kraków I discovered the power of moving pictures. Having somehow in my roamings come across a free movie theater—I certainly had no money—I saw two films. One was a Russian film about unhappy love, the name of which I no longer remember, or perhaps never knew (I did not yet read Russian), though I recall quite clearly its story and some of its scenes. A soldier on leave is on his way home to his village to thatch his mother's roof. As the train wends its way through vast sunny birch forests, he falls in love with a girl. Inevitably they must part, she to go her way, he to thatch the roof. As I watched, I couldn't help thinking of our endless musings, Tośka's and mine, about the unhappiness of true love. The other movie was *Gunga Din*. Based on a Rudyard Kipling poem, as I later learned, this well-known film is about an Indian uprising, brave British soldiers, and the scantily clad water carrier Gunga Din, who sacrifices his life to save the British soldiers. Since I knew neither English nor anything about India, most of the movie's content must have escaped me. But whether I understood or not was not important. It was the fantasy world on the screen that seemed so real, though I knew that it wasn't. I lost myself in the images of sun-drenched forests, of mountains, and of parched deserts, unable to distinguish the real from the imagined until the movie ended and I stumbled outside, trying to get my bearings once more in the actual world.

These films, however, were soon eclipsed by the far more powerful images of the Wawel, the royal castle of the Polish kings that once more brought the memory of Tośka to mind. One afternoon, after I had already explored the squares and churches on the way to Long Street and the soup kitchen, I decided to go in the opposite direction, down Grodzka Street. It was a long walk, and after taking two turns, left and right, I found myself on Kanoniczna Street. Suddenly before me like a wonderful design on a magic carpet was the Wawel—the castle, the cathedral, the gates, and the Wawel's many other buildings. It seemed to be a vision and I was afraid it might disappear when I looked away.

My feet carried me in the direction of the Wawel—it attracted me like a magnet. Finally I stood in the great courtyard, though I couldn't say how I got there. The courtyard was overgrown with weeds, and heaps of rubbish were everywhere, but that afternoon I didn't see the neglect. My eyes were glued to the magnificent buildings, the castle with its arcades and columns, its windows and parapets. My imagination conjured up images of kings and queens behind those windows, watching carriages that came and went. Maids-in-waiting, hiding behind heavy curtains, looked down on their beloved knights preparing to leave on important missions. I could see grooms and servants rushing to and fro, waiting on important personages. I conjured up messengers arriving with communications from far-flung courts, their horses glistening with sweat from the long, hard ride. I thought I still heard the pounding of their hooves on the cobblestones and the rumbling of carriage wheels, the shouted orders, the servants' rapid footsteps. The past echoed in the neglected courtyard, a past that wasn't mine, but one that I so very much wanted to be mine and that I had come to know a little in the novels by Henryk Sienkiewicz that Tośka and I had read in another time and place.

I left the Wawel enclosure and made my way down to the river's edge and lay on the grass along the riverbank. The day was overcast and under gray skies the blue water seemed gray too. The countryside on the bank across from me was desolate and empty. Seen from the river's edge, the Wawel, with its stark turrets, towers, and domes, had become a brooding fortress that guarded the river and the countryside beyond. The rows of windows facing the Vistula River seemed like so many eyes watching me down below. I felt threatened, as if someone were standing behind those windows following my every move; perhaps not even a living person, a ghost, someone who was wronged and wanted revenge. I stared hard at each window in turn but they were all quite empty. There was no sound, except the gentle murmur of the Vistula.

In the weeks that followed I went almost daily to the Wawel. I would sit at the river's edge and on sunny days watch the lazily drifting clouds in the blue sky, or look at the shiny pebbles in the sparkling water. I would then see ships sailing downriver to the king's court, ships on which valiant knights returned from distant expeditions, or which brought eagerly awaited envoys on diplomatic missions. Court ladies crowded the windows of the castle; they watched the ships anchor in the bend of the river. Then a procession of noblemen and servants slowly wound its way up to the ramparts of the great castle.

Again I went into the courtyard, listening to the sounds of bygone days—a royal wedding perhaps, the king's youngest daughter about to be married to a foreign prince. The guests are arriving for the grand celebration and carriages laden with gifts roll into the courtyard. Crowds of peasants who have come from near and far watch the festive preparations openmouthed. Soon the bells of the great cathedral will begin to peal, announcing the start of the royal procession to the cathedral. Delicious smells of roasting geese and rising breads come from the royal kitchen, on the ground floor of the castle.

Time passed swiftly for me in such reveries and only the sun's progress reminded me to hurry home before darkness fell. One afternoon I saw more visitors in the courtyard. Groups of peasant women and city people stood looking at the castle and its secretive windows and doors. Some entered hesitantly through a low doorway. I followed them. And then I saw the tapestries. In a subterranean room they covered the walls from ceiling to floor. And now I too stood openmouthed. I had never seen anything like this, never imagined that anything like these tapestries existed. At first I thought they were paintings, huge, larger-than-life paintings of wonderful pastoral scenes. But when I looked closer I saw that they were made of woven material. Or were they? No, I decided, they were embroidered—millions of tiny stitches made by the finest needles with the thinnest of yarns by thousands of maidens, year after year. Hadn't Tośka once told me something like that?

Still, for me it wasn't so much how they were made, nor was it the stories they apparently told and the scenes they depicted. It was their size, their grandeur, their majesty that were riveting. There were meadows and gardens, or perhaps parks, green vegetation and flowering trees. A bubbling brook divided a peaceful landscape; a sleepy village hovered on the horizon. There were birds in the trees, small animals on the ground, playful dogs, patient donkeys, an occasional horse with a flowing mane. Splendid peacocks moved in lush vegetation, vines clung to trees, and in the distance were gently rolling hills. Here was perpetual spring without the withering cold of winter's snow and frost. Here was tranquility and peace. Along the borders were other scenes: playful monkeys and fantastic birds, many different kinds of fruit—grapes and lemons, peaches and plums. Among flowering plants strange beings played instruments or nodded in peaceful sleep.

Never before had I encountered this kind of art, beauty transformed into tangible image. St. Mary's was wonderful, its soaring height inspiring, its stained-glass windows forever revealing something never before seen. But these tapestries were different. Someone with boundless imagination had taken the real world of flowers, plants, animals, and people and had transformed it into an ideal world without hunger and fear, arrested in a moment of perfection.

I couldn't stop thinking about the tapestries from then on. Celina's mother's scolding voice reached my ears occasionally, but whatever it was she was saying did not register. I heard the conversations around the dinner table as if from a great distance. Before my mind's eye were only the landscapes from which war had been banished. For me the tapestries became the garden— now vastly enlarged—where I had played as a child, the garden that had vanished and from which I had disappeared. I still went to the soup kitchen every day and waited my turn in the ever-growing queue; I heard the complaining voices and the mournful Treblinka tune. Yet these sounds too came as if from a great distance, and when someone spoke to me I often stared stupidly. I hadn't heard a thing.

More than before, I lost track of time. I walked through the grounds of the Wawel, sometimes peeked into the cathedral, but for the most part I sat in the courtyard daydreaming, or stood in front of the tapestries, minutely examining each detail. Throughout the weeks of fantasizing about the life of the castle until the day of my discovery of the tapestries, I had never entered the castle. Now I began to wonder what else there might be inside, and eventually I followed some people who, whispering to one another, climbed up the great staircase to the second-floor landing. I didn't know what further wonders to expect. Were there more tapestries, perhaps, or other treasures that defied imagination? I was not prepared for what I found.

The rooms upstairs were barren. Refuse littered the floor. The walls were dirty, and they had ugly holes, bloodless wounds where large chunks of plaster had been gouged out. Seen from the inside, the windows that had sparkled in the afternoon sun when I looked up at them from the river's edge were blind with dirt. The summer's dust and rain had left ugly streaks. I walked from room to room; one after another, each had damaged floors, ruined walls, an overturned chair, a badly scratched table. Each room was empty, with no sign of its glorious past. The exhilaration of the previous weeks gave way to distress. War and pillage had also come to these royal rooms. Nothing was spared. Only the splendid tapestries remained. Ugly and stark emptiness above contrasted sharply with the beauty below.

SEPTEMBER 1980

Returning to Poland for the first time many years later, I begin my journey to Mielec and into the past in Kraków and with the Wawel. Despite the passage of time, I have not forgotten the tapestries and my first encounter with history. I go to the Wawel exactly as I had that first time: from the Main Market along Grodzka Street, then up steep Kanoniczna to the Wawel itself. Grodzka, once part of the important trade route from Hungary to Western Europe, is now a pleasant thoroughfare of shops and restaurants. But these do not interest me. I hurry to see the tapestries, still convinced after all these years that hundreds of castle maidens had embroidered them, adding stitch to tiny stitch, year after year. The tapestries are displayed in the wonderfully restored Hall of Senators with its brightly colored ceiling; the neglect I had seen in 1945 is now past and forgotten. Shining chandeliers and standing lamps illuminate the great hall and the tapestries—and they are as breathtaking as they were the first time I saw them. For a moment I am again that lost teenager totally enchanted by the magnificence, the amazing beauty of these hangings. But when I examine them closely I discover (my heart sinking) that they are not embroidered. They are woven. The posted description informs me that more than 140 tapestries were produced in the sixteenth century in Flemish workshops, which at the time were famous for the quality of their workmanship and materials. They were created at the request of King Sigismund Augustus Jagiełło, who is known to have been an art connoisseur. So that is their story. But I am not yet ready to accept this version of events. I don't want to think of the tapestries as business, as bought and paid for; I want to hold on to my fantasy of castle maidens who created these beautiful designs. Much as I try, I also cannot tell whether the tapestries I am seeing now are the ones I saw then. How many had there been in that room below the castle? As many as there are now in this hall? The tapestries in the Hall of Senators portray scenes familiar from the Bible: Adam and Eve, Noah and the Ark, the Tower of Babel. Wouldn't I recognize and know now if these were the ones I saw?

Is the past then a mirage, memory always inaccurate and

blurred, the tapestries imagined rather than seen? I learn later that when the Germans invaded Poland in September 1939, the tapestries together with other Wawel treasures were put on a barge and sent down the Vistula, then loaded on a hay wagon and thereafter into cars for the journey to Rumania. From Rumania they were shipped to Aubusson in France. French restorers worked on those tapestries that had suffered damage en route until Germany invaded France, and then the Wawel treasures were hurriedly sent to England. Since England at the time was under heavy German bombardment, by good fortune the Polish ocean liner *Batory* was able to take the priceless tapestries to Canada immediately. And in Canada they remained until they were returned to Poland in 1961.

CHAPTER SIX

CHOICES

So: She survived the war, finished her studies, married.

She collected things: old and new documents, photographs, examination results, postcards, bills, receipts, prayers, newspaper clippings. . . . Everything to her became the past. Her organism produced the past with amazing rapidity.

She was drawn to people. She repelled them with her . . . irony, exaggeratedly begged forgiveness and again sought them out. . . . She feared loneliness, illness, cold, neighbors, dogs, people looking strangely at her, others' opinions, her own fears. . . .

HANNA KRALL, *There Is No Longer a River*

(Da ist kein Fluss mehr)

It's strange how clear the memory of that fateful July morning still is. There was a gray, cool dawn, a fine drizzle in the air as Mother, Sister, and I walked through Kraków's deserted streets, the houses on both sides of the street secretive with their closed windows, almost sinister in the morning dawn. Then, near the railroad station, crowds of people hurried past with their bundles. Some had suitcases secured with twine, no doubt "organized" (as Sister used to say, that is, appropriated along the way) while others had tied huge bundles to their back, knotting them in front over one shoulder. Singly or in groups, they hurried along to the train. Everyone was going somewhere, everyone having come from elsewhere: Polish laborers returning home from Germany; Hungarians and Rumanians leaving Poland; young men and women freed from concentration camps looking for some family, for someone who might still be alive. And then there were those who restlessly just needed to keep moving, knowing already that they no longer had either home or family. These were scenes not unlike those I had seen when Sister and I traveled to Kraków.

A huge crowd seethed inside the gloomy station and outside on the platform, waiting impatiently for the train's arrival. No one asked where it was going, as long as it was going somewhere. And when at last it arrived with its closed cattle cars and open platform cars, the people hurled themselves on it as if no other train would ever come to take them to unknown destinations. They pushed and shoved and soon filled every available space, even on the coal car, on the locomotive, and on the couplings, while still others tried to get on, hauled aboard by their comrades. Although the crowd on the platform had thinned out, the crush on the train caused by latecomers continued.

We three stood on the platform, holding on to our small bundles of provisions for the journey, afraid of losing one another in the surging crowd. We wanted to get on the train—it was headed toward Prague, or so we thought—but we knew there was little chance of doing so without being separated. As we stood there, fearfully wondering what to do, several Russian soldiers in freshly laundered uniforms made their leisurely way to the only passenger car on the train. Respectfully, the crowd was clearing a path for them, when suddenly the unexpected happened. Seeing the three of us standing there helplessly, neither moving forward nor able to retreat, one of the soldiers took hold of us as if we were long-lost friends and, pushing and pulling, propelled us into their compartment. Mother, not realizing quite what had happened, seemed hesitant, but Sister and I settled happily into comfortable seats. It was a simple, yet very meaningful, human gesture, a help-ing hand, as if it portended a new beginning.

Our journey was long but well-planned by Mother and her friends in Kraków. We had papers that would allow us to travel as far as Prague. In Prague, it had been decided, we were to get papers for Linz, Austria, which was still in the Russian-occupied zone. No one would suspect that we would then head for the American-occupied zone. Exactly how we would cross from the Russian zone to the American zone was not clear. We would find out in Prague. Our ultimate destination was Frankfurt, where Mother hoped to find her youngest sister, Friedel. Friedel's non-Jewish husband, Arno, was a communist, which was, to be sure, undesirable in Nazi Germany, but better than being Jewish. Chances were that she hadn't been deported and killed and that both were alive.

The train rolled through the lush Polish countryside, through green meadows and ripening wheat fields dotted with red poppies. Was I thinking of the past, of Tośka perhaps, whom I had always wanted to introduce to the red poppies, but never did? Did I have hopes, expectations? Did I regret leaving Poland? Perhaps I was so caught up in the adventure of the journey that neither the known past nor the unknown future mattered much. I call it an adventure because before long we came to a halt. The Russians vanished and all those who had so valiantly fought for a tiny space on the train now settled down on the station's platform to wait for the next train, which presumably would carry us a little closer to our destination. And so it went, throughout bright sunny days and star-studded nights—waiting in stations of name-less towns, pushing, elbowing our way onto the next train, until at last we crossed the Czech border.

The countryside was no different—rolling hills, small orchards, fields planted in grain and potatoes, clusters of tiny villages with houses surrounded by picket fences and ripening sunflowers turning their faces to the sun. What was different across the border was that kindly villagers and townspeople came to the station with large canisters of milk, cauldrons of soup, and thick slices of fragrant black bread. They led us to the water pump in their yards and made us wash the black soot off our faces. Thirst quenched, hunger stilled, accompanied by kind smiles and good wishes, we waited for the next train.

On the rainy evening of July 6, 1945, we arrived in Prague. As in Kraków, the station was filled to overflowing with people, arriving, departing, crowding the platforms; people rushing off purposefully to wherever they were going. Again we three stood in the station, not knowing what to do next, where to spend the night, where to get the documents for further travel, whom to ask and how. I could understand some Czech, which is somewhat similar to Polish, but not enough to understand street directions in an unfamiliar city. Then, just as in Kraków, help came unexpectedly: A man appeared, holding a piece of cherry cake, having apparently spotted us for the helpless strangers we were. Had he been about to eat the cherry cake, but then thought better of it when he saw us? Or did he come each day to the station with a piece of cherry cake? Whatever the case, and I have often thought of this cherry cake–bearing man, he gave it to me (I hope I shared it with both Mother and Sister) and I ate this most delicious of cakes slowly, savoring each bite's sweet, tangy flavor. The man then led us through dark streets to a large building (a school perhaps), delivered us into the hands of some people who eagerly wielded DDT guns, and promised to return the following morning. It was our first encounter with DDT powder; our hosts no doubt made the correct assumption that anyone coming from Poland at that time was infested with vermin. Sprayed repeatedly thereafter, we eventually ceased to be surprised by this evidence of Western progress, and accepted delousing as a fact of life.

The man did indeed return the following day to take us to the Czechoslovak repatriation office, where large numbers of people were already waiting for travel documents. These, it turned out, were easily arranged. After Mother produced her release papers from Schindler's Brünlitz camp, dated May 15, 1945, which stated that she'd been a political concentration camp prisoner, she was issued a registration certificate according to which she was not only five years younger but had also metamorphosed into a German Jew going home. We didn't, after all, have to pretend we wanted to go to Linz, for according to our new documents we were returning to Frankfurt. Like the officials, the certificate was friendly; the bearer was admonished to "Keep it at all times to assist your safe return home!" Joined by four other people, a couple and their grown daughter and a youngish single man, we were to travel to Pilsen, and there cross over to the American zone where a DP (displaced persons) camp was already functioning. How very efficiently the Czechs had arranged everything. Or was this already the work of the Brichah, the organization that eventually moved the masses of homeless and dispossessed Jews across borders?

Once again we boarded a train—this time it was no cattle car. We traveled to Pilsen, walked to the border, showed our documents to the Russian soldiers and then to the Americans (the latter were more interested in spraying us with DDT than in examining our papers), and then crossed over.

We may not have spent much longer than two or three weeks in this border DP camp (it may have been the Karlov camp), yet for me those unhurried, quiet days were a calm way station. The camp was actually an abandoned convent with vast grounds and green lawns under old shade trees. The gleaming white buildings—the nuns' quarters, I assumed—were locked, and the camp population, increasing daily, was housed in temporary barracks. There was nothing to do. We didn't even have to worry about food. Three times a day, hefty German women wheeled a large cauldron of either thin soup or mashed potatoes from the kitchen to the barracks. We despised the Germans, convinced that they were SS women, ex–concentration camp guards, since even on the hottest days they wore long-sleeved blouses to hide the SS tattoos we were sure they had on their arms. Although they knew who we were, they nonetheless were arrogant, and we cursed them under our breath. Bread was in short supply, and wanting to supplement our unvarying diet, I made occasional forays into the surrounding villages through a hole in the fence. The farmers were generous and I always returned with a pot of the cheese for which this region is famous. Once, I remember, I traded an old roll of film Sister had mysteriously found somewhere for a chocolate bar from American soldiers. But these brief excursions were neither mandatory— we did not go hungry—nor did they take much time.

The camp's surroundings seemed to hold nothing of interest and I often daydreamed in the grass under a tree or in the bright sun. I imagined hearing the church bells call the nuns to prayer, seeing them walk slowly toward the chapel in the shade of the white walkways, fingering their rosaries. I imagined them at their various tasks, sweeping, cleaning vegetables, cooking, or sitting in quiet contemplation. I didn't know where these nuns were now, who had made them leave their peaceful convent. Perhaps they were reduced to wandering without a home, as we were. Surely they were bound to return someday, whereas I would never go home again. I had no home to go to, and with each day Poland receded farther into a dim past where once I had been. Mielec had become part of another time. Poznań, school, the Orlowskys, even Kraków's churches and the Wawel, seemed to belong to another existence. But I did not want to think—not of the past, not of Tośka, not of Cousin Esther, who I knew was dead, nor of

Father's song. I wanted to think only of now and what might take place tomorrow.

I was never left long to my daydreams. Our room in the barracks was acquiring the strong smell of ripening cheese and to escape it one or another of our roommates would take to roaming the convent grounds, finding me eventually somewhere in the tall grass. Until the next round of mashed potatoes, we would while away the time talking about the hated SS women. Now it is us against them, we said, not them against us. And we are the strong ones, as they will soon find out. Isn't it wonderful that we no longer need to be afraid of them?

Slowly I learned to relate to strangers, trying to see myself as they saw me, an adolescent, not yet an adult but no longer a child. I enjoyed these light, noncommittal talks; we were traveling companions on this one brief journey only, and would soon part, never to meet again. Being with them, stranded in limbo, in a curious way allowed the forging of a tentative new relationship among Mother, Sister, and myself. I realized this only much later. We three, we were a family then . . . and yet we weren't. How could we be without Father? We never mentioned him, never talked about him, but his absence was with us, and the true sense of belonging together as a family grew gradually only much later in America, when we thought for a time that maybe we could be like other people, or were expected to be.

At last we were leaving the camp for Germany. A long convoy of trucks arrived, driven by clean-cut American soldiers. We rode the entire day, stopping only once in a forest, where we picked wonderfully sweet wild strawberries, while much to our amusement the American soldiers tossed a little ball back and forth. Later I would learn about this game and eventually learned that it was baseball practice.

Toward evening we came to Regensburg. Some of us were left

off at a convent from which, unlike the previous one, the nuns had not departed. They received us hospitably, gave us food, and then took us to a large ward. In long rows of beds were men and women older than I had ever seen; wizened, pale old faces peered at us from clean sheets, the old people smiling toothless smiles and stretching out wrinkled hands in welcome. Proudly the nuns told us that they had rescued these Jewish men and women (perhaps from Theresienstadt) and were now caring for them. We walked among the beds, holding this one's then that one's hand, hugging and kissing the old people, knowing that these fragile souls were a precious remnant we might not see anywhere else again. We could not imagine how they had survived when the very old and the very young alike had been killed. Today I think that meeting these old men and women at the end of our journey, when a new future was still only a barely imagined possibility, was also strangely symbolic of a past already lost to us.

We went down into the streets and looked at the incredible destruction from Allied bombing. The convent seemed to be the only building that had escaped the devastation. There were shells of burned-out buildings everywhere; on some the front had collapsed, revealing rooms precariously hanging in midair. Streets had disappeared under the rubble of collapsed buildings. Here and there, old people shifted stones and bricks in search of their belongings. They were shabby and unkempt, but I felt no pity for them. Again I thought, as I often would in the months to come: You can no longer harm me; I walk among you and I'm not afraid. Nor do I have to pretend anymore that I am someone else.

A couple, a young man wearing immaculate white trousers and white shirt and a young woman, both a stark contrast to the Germans rummaging for things they once owned, were coming toward us. "*Amkha,*" they said. It was the first time I heard this greeting, but I knew at once what it meant: *Amkha,* we're of the same people, we may belong nowhere, but we belong together. Later I often heard this word exchanged when Jewish strangers met (are you one of ours?), and when the answer was *amkha* there would be noisy greetings, as if old friends had found one another by chance. Inexplicably, my memory has forged together the realization of fear's absence, the meeting with the old men and women, and that greeting during the first afternoon in Germany. Kuba, the young man who said the word, and I became close friends for less than a year and then he disappeared, as would all of my friends.

From my diary:

> July 23, 1945: I traveled from Poland to Germany. A new world opened, unknown to me until now and despised. It sounds silly, but my thoughts have not enough room in my head.
>
> July 24, 1945: If only I had someone to talk with about all this, I would feel easier. I am lonely for Poland.
>
> August 1, 1945: Life is without content, it disgusts me. They only think about beautiful dresses and I am so lonely. . . .

Reconstructing those first weeks and months in Germany isn't easy. The weeks of solitude in Kraków, when I was left to my own devices except for the daily chore of fetching soup, then the quiet, restful days at the Pilsen convent-camp, had suddenly given way to a household of little-known relatives, Aunt Friedel and her husband Arno, and their friends and visitors at their house in Frankfurt.

Friedel had indeed survived the war, sheltered by the German underground. Arno, a well-known journalist, was incarcerated toward the end of the war in a labor camp. According to one ver-

sion of Friedel's story, as soon as the Americans arrived in Frankfurt, she told them to find her husband, who could immediately
commence publishing a newspaper, which would help normalize
the situation. They could trust him; he hadn't been a Nazi, she
assured the Americans.

Friedel, who was a formidably persuasive lady, also said that
she and her husband would need a place to live. Presumably the
Americans told her to choose any house she wished and to move
in, which is exactly what she did. The house she selected was an
elegant three-story structure with a wood-paneled foyer and a spiral staircase leading from the first to the second floor. The third
floor had burned down, and Sister and her friends called it the
sundeck. The foyer and staircase had red carpeting. On the second floor, one entire room consisted of wardrobes and mirrors,
and there was a sunken marble bathtub in the bathroom. There
were six of us in the house, including Eva, who was about Sister's
age. Eva was not part of the family, but she had met Friedel, or
perhaps it was Arno, somewhere and, having nowhere to go, had
come to live with them.

The house was located in what recently must have been an
exclusive part of the city, but in 1945 was, like the rest of Frankfurt, mostly in ruins. The destruction was nearly complete. As in
Regensburg, thick rubble covered entire streets; in partially collapsed houses rooms hung grotesquely in midair together with
their overturned furniture. This new and unknown world was an
uncomfortable place in which I had no function, no sense of
belonging, but where I could no longer follow my own inclina-
tions. Fixed routines continued, new routines were quickly established. Mother again stood at the stove cooking soups and
vegetables and, as in Kraków, she squinted myopically into the
pots, her face still drawn and sad. It would be several months
before she finally got glasses. Each morning, Friedel mounted her

bicycle and went off in search of food. For many weeks we had mostly cucumbers, which Mother transformed into soups and strange-tasting vegetable dishes. Arno worked in his study with the American press advisers or, in the afternoons, with Friedel, who did all his typing. Eva's friends visited and the girls went up to the sundeck.

I soon found a place for myself on the spiral staircase; from there I could hear the girls upstairs and watch what was going on downstairs. Eva was in love with Larry, the handsome American who worked with Arno. He wore horn-rimmed glasses and had a serious face. Larry spoke German, his parents having left Germany for America before the war, which was why he was assigned to help Arno. Eva was sure he was as much in love with her as she with him, and that he would somehow find a way to bring her to America. Perhaps Larry had promised, but most likely she just wanted to believe it. Her friend Hanna, who spent most of her days at the house, was in love with an Italian-American soldier; in fact, as it turned out, she was pregnant by him. Like Eva, Hanna was absolutely certain that her boyfriend, who was not Jewish and whom we never met, would take her with him to America.

The sundeck talk was all about love and marriage and how life would be wonderful in America. The girls seldom talked of the past; only occasionally would someone mention an incident in one concentration camp or another where they had been. Mostly there was only the present and what was yet to be, together with their love for those tall, handsome soldiers, who like fairy-tale princes would transport them to a magic land. Marriage to an "Ami," an American soldier, that summer seemed the only alternative to remaining in Germany.

Downstairs the talk was all business: how the *Frankfurter Rundschau,* the paper Arno was about to start, must become a medium for conveying democratic values; how editorials must be separated from factual reporting; how to procure paper; how to arrange for printing presses; how to meet the deadline for the first issue. Americans in clean, pressed uniforms and shiny boots came and went with bulging briefcases. To me they seemed like supermen, tall, athletic, well-fed men from a different planet. Sometimes one or another visitor deigned to speak to us. I was overcome by confusion when one Englishman from the British zone said he thought that having been hidden was novel, interesting, and seldom heard. Was he already bored by too much concentration camp talk?

When we met around the kitchen table for the noonday meal the talk turned to politics: Germany's future, the Allied occupation, what might be expected once the Nuremberg trials of the war criminals got under way in November. Arno was still a Marxist, although he no longer belonged to the Communist Party. Often, while eating Mother's latest cucumber creation, we would hear a lecture on the exploitation of the proletariat and the inevitable demise of capitalism, notwithstanding Arno's undisguised admiration for American democracy. Tall, slim, and soft-spoken, his dark eyes twinkling behind glasses, Arno argued persuasively for joining Marxism with democratic institutions. Not so Friedel, who was a more dogmatic Marxist than he. She passionately championed the rights of the proletariat and in no uncertain terms expressed her contempt for the bourgeoisie, to which, she said, we three belonged. Energetically brushing her short hair back from her round face, she accused us of having been indifferent to the plight of poor workers and the underprivileged.

It may have been Friedel's vehemence with its outright hostility to Christianity and religion generally that disturbed me, for on August 7 I noted in my diary: "The Communist Party is not Christian? How can this be, when the goal is to help those nearby, which is also a Christian goal?" And on August 13: "Communism is not against the Church, only against the priests." These are, to be sure, the naive observations of a fifteen-year-old who had, moreover, brought with her the belief, prevalent in those early years after Poland was liberated by the Russian army, that a compromise between Church and communist ideology was possible. But now Friedel had raised the question of religion as "the opium of the people." No wonder I wrote in my diary that I wished for someone I could truly open up to, ask questions of—someone with whom I could sort out these matters of belief.

In the afternoons, the kitchen and the kitchen table were commandeered by the girls and their dressmaking enterprise. Sister, having learned dressmaking before the war, was in charge. Old dresses were taken apart and new ones produced from them. The talk now was of fashions, fabrics, and colors that matched or didn't; of what best suited a dark or a light complexion. Eva, who had black hair, honey-colored skin, and lively gray eyes, liked tight dresses that showed off her slim figure. She was good-looking and vivacious, and she firmly believed in dressing fashionably. Hanna was short and more graceful than Eva, but she was already beginning to gain weight and was most in need of new clothes. Where Eva was strong and tough (although she may not always have been that way), Hanna with her large eyes and short, curly hair seemed gentle and weak. The dressmaking activities were heartily supported by Friedel, who wanted to see us return to "civilized" life. I found this puzzling. Life in Germany did not strike me as especially civilized, nor could a pretty dress disguise uncivilized behavior. But eventually I too came to be fashionably attired in a skirt and an Eisenhower jacket—a style modeled on American army uniforms that had become quite the rage. Friedel also took the three of us to the hairdresser's, where she gleefully ordered my braids cut off, having hated them from the moment we arrived. After many hours, the hairdresser had transformed our stringy, dull hair into frizzy permanents. Mother and Sister seemed pleased with their new looks. I wasn't at all sure; the braids had been part of my Polish self. What was my self now with a frizzy hair style? During those first weeks we paid much attention to hair and teeth, for both had suffered from neglect and malnutrition.

Sometimes I joined the girls in the kitchen, listening to their interminable chatter about fashions and dresses. Her chores done, Mother would sit with us and unravel old sweaters for reknitting into bathing suits. Unfortunately, she hadn't considered that the wool, being old, would be weak and would unravel when the stitches became waterlogged. None of us told her, not even Friedel, who seldom minced her words and who was often oblivious to her elder sister's grief. As I reflect on the dynamics among us four incompatible women, I am amazed that for a few months at least we managed to get along without major clashes.

An alliance gradually evolved between Friedel and Sister, who became increasingly dependent on this strong woman. Sister's growing need to lean on someone (actively encouraged by Friedel) may have been due to her slowly developing illness, eventually diagnosed as tuberculosis. At the same time, Friedel was ever more displeased with me—somehow I was not the way I ought to be—while Mother moved among us distant, as if sleepwalking; she was there, but part of her was still elsewhere and the hunted look seldom left her face. Mother's remoteness together with my adolescent confusion and occasional defiance must have exasperated Friedel, for we both eluded her attempts at control and her strong desire to be needed by each of us. No wonder I frequently wrote in my diary that I felt sad and wished I could leave, go far, far away, never to see Germany and Germans again. My strong dislike of Germans fused with my growing conviction that I should be other than I was. But being contrary by nature, instead of trying to please Friedel, to become perhaps more pliant to her will, I did exactly the opposite. For a time, it was Arno who seemed to understand better than she that because I had once saved myself from certain death, obediently dependent behavior could not be expected of me. He had a compassionate heart.

We did not talk about Poland, except once, shortly after we had arrived. After supper, under the soft overhead kitchen light, Arno, Friedel, and we three sat around the kitchen table. Arno asked us, one by one, to tell what had happened. And so we did, summarizing in the course of a few evening hours six years of living and dying, six lost years. A few months later, Arno wrote an editorial about us in the new publication *Frankfurter Rundschau,* retelling our experiences and contrasting them with those of a German youth. Reading this editorial today, I see how even then—a mere four months after the war's end—events, sequences of events, were already subtly changed, had not happened in quite the way Arno wrote about them. Even then merely retelling the story was not enough. But perhaps I've got it all wrong and Arno's is the correct version. Perhaps half a century later it is my memory that is inaccurate. On the other hand, Arno's purpose in writing this editorial was not to tell a story of persecution and suffering. Rather he intended to show how an entire generation of German youths blindly followed without questioning. The message, not memory, is what mattered to Arno.

Much had changed by the end of summer. Mother's periodic visits to Jewish organizations in search of relatives had paid off. First, a "cousin" (as long as they were Geminders we called them cousins), Hayim Geminder, turned up. He belonged to the other branch of the Geminders, who had lived on the Small Market, and we, in fact, had not known him in Mielec. He was a short fellow who for some unknown reason wore a dark blue uniform and who owned a large "machine," as motorcycles were called then. He dealt on the black market. His merchandise included wristwatches that he wore (as had Russian soldiers) on both arms up to the elbow. He became a regular visitor at the house, sometimes bringing us the fruits of his illegal transactions. Though we should have been morally obliged to reject these ill-gotten gifts, even the most high-minded person would have found it hard to resist a package of tea or the even more treasured coffee. Second, and more important, the husband of Father's sister Sheindl—that is, Mother's brother-in-law—turned up in Bavaria. He was the only member of the Padawer family who survived. Still, Mother, having finally gotten glasses, squinted less and seemed a little more animated. Aside from her two sisters in Bolivia and two brothers in Argentina, Hayim (Heinrich) Padawer was the only close member of our family, and the only one on Father's side, who had survived. But we still had hopes in 1945 (and even later) that a niece or nephew, or one of Mother's other sisters, might turn out to be alive and suddenly appear at our doorstep.

By the end of summer I overcame my aversion to moving about in Frankfurt, this ugly ruined city with its collapsed buildings. Not wanting to be identified as German, I pinned a blue-and-white stripe to my dress, as I had seen other Jews do, and I was glad when Germans looked at me disdainfully. I wanted them to know that I was Jewish and that they hadn't succeeded in killing me. When meeting one of "our" people for the first time, we would delightedly say *amkha* and become at once the closest of friends.

When a DP camp—actually no more than many barracks in a large field—was established in nearby Zeilsheim, I began to spend most days of the week there. On August 29, I wrote in my diary that the food in Zeilsheim was very good. I didn't mention the

ugly barracks, or the mud when it rained. By registering in Zeilsheim I drew rations at the camp. Friedel welcomed the additional
food and for once I felt I had done something right in her eyes. I
also made new friends, my first friends after my cherished friendship with Tośka.

In Zeilsheim's bleak barracks, sitting on hard makeshift beds,
we talked about communism, about equality for all, and especially about whether or not to go to Eretz Israel. Was it not our
land, the only place where we could be at home? Palestine must be
for the Jews, I wrote in my diary on August 19; on September 3, I
wrote that I probably would be going there. Perhaps sometimes I
still might have thought of becoming a nun, of seeking a quiet,
selfless life dedicated to higher causes; perhaps when I was lonely,
when the confusion of people felt oppressive, when I sought the
solitude that was so hard to come by. But I was glad to be with my
new friends, glad to discuss new ideas, and above all glad to speak
Polish with them instead of German. And while I still occasionally longed for Poland, especially for the ordered life I had led for
a short time with the Orlowskys in Poznań, being Jewish with
other Jews—all of them so different—was increasingly comfortable. I often marvel today at the ease, the effortlessness, with
which I became one or another person; the ease with which I
changed from a pious Jewish girl to an equally pious Catholic
one, and then to a secular Jewish one. Yet these were not days of
introspection, and what mattered was being alive.

Not everyone could stand DP camp life, living in a barracks
again, subject to the rules and regulations considered necessary by
the Americans who ran the camps. By the beginning of autumn,
when the weather was turning colder, I discovered a small group
of young people—most of them from Kraków or Warsaw—in a
dilapidated small hotel in the center of town. Like my friends in
Zeilsheim, they were in their early twenties, older than I by some

years, but they were more sophisticated and some had been university students. Apparently they had simply taken over this small, neglected place, most likely abandoned after an air raid. The rooms were gloomy and unkempt, the hallways dark and musty; dirty dishes were stacked everywhere, sometimes entangled with dirty laundry; but my friends were as cheerful as a flock of birds temporarily alighted on a less than tidy tree. As far as they were concerned, anything was better than yet another camp.

Their discussions differed from those of my Zeilsheim friends. Yes, Palestine was an option, but right now there were more pressing questions, they believed. How did it happen (for surely it was not we who had caused it to happen), they asked, that we were here, that we were spared, that we were alive? Were we stronger, smarter, better (for the first time in my life I heard mention of Darwin), or were we in fact meaner, more ruthless, more selfish than those who perished? Why were we spared? Or was our being here as senseless, as empty of any meaning as all our terrible experiences? They talked and questioned while I listened and asked. In between, overcome by hunger, we would go out into the foggy, wet streets to find food. Remembering now the intensity with which these half dozen or so young men and women attempted to bring reason to bear on the question "Why me?"—why not my sister, my brother, my friend?—I don't seem to remember that we also talked about God. I don't think we were concerned with God's designs, unlike many theologians and educators today, or with why He didn't save His chosen people from calamity. Perhaps we were too preoccupied with our own survival and its meaning for our lives in the future. Perhaps it was enough to know that the catastrophe had not been averted. Why bother speculating about theological reasons it hadn't?

After all these years I can still see our little group in the chilly hotel room. We sat on the unmade beds with their rumpled gray sheets, wearing coats and mufflers and talking as if our lives depended on it. Now that we're here, that we're alive, shouldn't we understand what we must do? We were as if reborn—born, however, with all our senses. We could make choices, not what to do, seek success, riches, contentment, but about what kind of person to be. We could consciously choose who and what we wanted to be. To mindlessly live day in, day out would never do. Being alive instead of all those others who died, we now also had responsibilities not only to ourselves but to the dead for whom we had to speak. What were these responsibilities, this burden we needed to assume? Gradually I learned about freedom and choices, and that living implied assuming responsibilities. I also realized how we, who had returned to life, could never live lives like others who were not where we had been.

That autumn I wrote a poem that seems clumsy to me now, but perhaps interesting because it tries to say something about escape while indicating its impossibility:

Wet shapes, wet lights
crowd my vision,
nature's forces hold sway
according to their design.
Afloat in a small puddle, I behold
a leaf like a boat;
with autumn's finest tinge
it still glistens red.
At times we dream a fairy tale,
have wings and drift
in life's large glass.

During that rainy and foggy autumn, I went less frequently to Zeilsheim, both because I was spending most of my time with

my friends in the hotel and because the camp was becoming unbelievably crowded with new arrivals daily pouring into the American zone. The food was no longer tasty, nor were the portions
sufficiently large. The barracks, ugly in summer, were now dark
and damp; the whole place was a gigantic mud puddle where
black marketeering was thriving and where the Americans openly
showed their contempt for the DPs. Most of my friends who had
been there at the end of summer had left, gone elsewhere to
escape the camp's hopeless atmosphere. Smooth-talking emissaries were busily recruiting young people for illegal emigration to
Palestine; their hard-sell tactics were not always convincing. I still
went occasionally to the dances organized in the camp. But after
a boy (I distinctly remember that he had bushy red hair) told me I
danced like a diesel engine, I gave up these visits as well.

The Frankfurt house grew increasingly cold and Friedel in-
stalled a wood-burning stove in Arno's downstairs study. Coal
was unavailable and Friedel now searched energetically for wood.
Frankfurt's streets having again become passable, Arno had acquired a car and a driver, Hans. He was a cheerful fellow whose
participation in the hunt for wood we valued highly. Yet no matter how many logs the two managed to find, it never seemed
enough. We either huddled in the kitchen—warm when Mother
cooked—or tried unobtrusively to sit in a corner in the study.

My reading life had resumed in the summer (it had stopped
when Sister and I left Poznań), after Arno handed me *Das Kapi-
tal.* It was not exactly engrossing reading, given my scanty knowledge of nineteenth-century literary German, and after a foray
into Rosa Luxemburg's revolutionary life, I settled down in the
warm study with Stefan Zweig's short stories. Larry, the American press adviser, unaccustomed to suffering cold indoors, staked
out a territorial claim next to the stove and the wood bin whenever he came. While he fed the little stove generously, Friedel was

nearly in tears watching her precious logs disappear one after another. She didn't know, and I didn't tell her, how I (and Mother and Sister as well) looked forward to the days of glorious warmth when Larry worked with Arno.

Those were also the days of my first encounter with the power of literature, when I read Zweig's masterful story "Amok," which told of feelings, of passion beyond reason, of irrational obsession. I clearly remember the excitement I felt when reading this strange tale of the contradiction between duty and desire, told in the darkness of night during a sea voyage. Was it because I, Mother too and Sister, had forgotten how to express emotions, or perhaps did not dare to, had not the words? When half a century later I reencountered this story in Chinese translation, it was like finding an old, nearly forgotten friend who reminded me of days long ago.

Love did not flourish in this cold city. One day Larry caught the measles—or the mumps—and he was hospitalized in an isolation ward. Eva's dreams of America crashed like a house of cards after Larry either told her or wrote her that he was married. Larry had not quite recovered when the army shipped him back to America. Heartbroken, Eva disappeared for a time, coming back only once to tell us that she was off to Italy and from there to Eretz Israel. After losing both her lover and her American dream, Eva believed she no longer had other choices. America was closed to DPs, unless relatives with much-coveted affidavits took responsibility that a DP would not become a public burden. Eva, like many others, simply did not want to remain in Germany any longer. Hanna had disappeared earlier. Her Italian-American boyfriend and father of her unborn child was also married, it turned out. One day, his tour of duty completed, he left. She never heard from him again, learning only later from one of his friends that he was married and was gone for good. Hanna did not tell us what she would do, which choices, if any, she thought she had. She simply vanished. After all, one could not easily believe that one had choices when for many years there were none or a decision made could turn out to be fatal. Even our recently found cousin, Hayim Geminder, was gone one day, though not for reasons of disappointed love. His black market enterprise, it seems, had taken him to Italy, where he was promptly jailed. With people disappearing one after another, the time had come to leave this gray, cold city. I didn't want force of circumstances to determine my choices.

APRIL 2000

A considerable portion of Chinese poetry is devoted to friendship—not necessarily to singing praises about friendship's significance, but to partings and meetings, to longing for departed friends, to fretting about their whereabouts. I especially like this friendship poetry, perhaps because it has a familiar ring and makes me think of the many friends who were so close to me, but long ago went to wherever they had to go.

How moving are these lines by the ninth-century poet Wei Yingwu, which he addressed as a letter to Secretary Yuan:

> Sadly, sadly remote from kin and friends
> Drifting, drifting through mist and fog.
> . . . .
> Where shall we meet again
> When life's affairs are a boat on waves
> Coasting on swirls unceasingly?

Wei Yingwu knew that he was powerless to bring about a meeting with his friend; he knew that only by chance and not by design would the two of them ever meet.

Wang Wei, writing in the eighth century, doubted that his friend would return even after one year, and he presents their parting with an air akin to finality. Nature's constancy differs from human affairs and the meeting of friends cannot be taken for granted:

> Having seen you off through the mountains
> At day's end I shut the thatch door.
> When next year's spring grass greens
> Will you my precious friend return?

The joyful reunion of friends after decades of separation is described by Du Fu, also of the eighth century, who cannot help exclaiming when the impossible happens:

> For friends to meet in life
> Is like the meeting of morning and evening stars.

I am deeply affected each time I read these poems, for my friends who taught me so much (even if I learned their lessons imperfectly) eventually scattered. We still met occasionally for two, three years while we were in Germany, and each meeting was cause for celebration. But then we went our separate ways, for leaving Germany, leaving the DP camps, leaving condescending American or Jewish officials behind was what mattered. We gave each other our photographs, our likenesses, having inscribed them "to my dear friend" or "for everlasting memory" or "never to forget" or "fight for a better tomorrow," but we never saw one another again.

I still have the photographs: Ruth Prager, Kuba wearing his white pants, handsome DP policeman Romek, Leon Kochalski, cheerful Joseph Steinhoff, Elzbieta with her beautifully bleached hair. . . . Were we to meet again, would our meetings be as joyous and as bittersweet as those of my Chinese poets? Perhaps not. Then we had only one another, though I was the lucky one among us, still having my mother and sister. But in those brief two years we were to one another the families and friends we had lost in Tarnów, Kraków, Radomyśl, in Bełżec, Stutthof, Majdanek; it was before Auschwitz had become a metaphor, before we were labeled the nonindividualized, anonymous "survivors" of today. And yet I cannot help longing to meet one or two of my friends someday, hoping foolishly they might return to me a part of myself that was somehow misplaced between Zeilsheim and Jerusalem.

Cham was a small DP camp of only a few hundred people. Actually, it was hardly a camp, because the DPs either lived in the only hotel of the sleepy Bavarian town or had rooms in German houses. After Mother married her brother-in-law, Heinrich Padawer—an event both Sister and I felt happy about—she went to live in Cham, while Sister remained in Frankfurt. On and off I too lived in Cham, but like most of my friends in the spring and summer of 1946, I traveled restlessly between DP camps as if in search of something, though neither I nor anyone else knew what it was. Friedel may have been relieved when I left Frankfurt, though she did not at all approve of my freedom and my unsettled existence.

A photograph taken from a slight rise above Cham shows a pretty town nestled among gently rolling hills, with two-story houses under sloping roofs, plenty of trees, and two church steeples. It was far more pleasant than the crowded Landsberg camp nearby, and even better than Munich, where most of Jewish life took place. American soldiers were not stationed in town, and important visitors, like David Ben-Gurion, went to Landsberg and did not bother with Cham. If the Germans resented the camp, I did not feel it. Except for the landladies, we had little or no contact with the German population, which seemed to consist for the most part of sullen and shabbily dressed elderly people. Cham was a quiet town, disturbed only by our boys and their noisy, oversized motorcycles or the occasional American jeep. Cham was picturesque, and yet I often wondered about the ugly Nazi past that surely was hidden behind those windows with their colorful flower boxes and lace curtains. Where were the SS men and soldiers now who had lived in those rooms and then gone to war to kill and maim? I wondered.

The camp ran itself with little interference from outside. Its offices, presided over by dignified Dr. Nebel, were located in one of the larger buildings in the center of town. Elzbieta in her elegant Eisenhower-jacket suits did secretarial work, such as it was. Excitable Abie, whose strong body odor preceded him wherever he went, was the intermediary between the camp and UNRRA (the United Nations Relief and Rehabilitation Agency), which supplied (or sometimes didn't) all our needs.

By April the long winter was in retreat. Limbs painfully swollen from the winter cold slowly returned to their normal shape. And Passover was only a few weeks hence. Excitement in the camp ran high. The UNRRA officials had promised Abie a plentiful supply of matzoh from America, for this was our first Passover as a free people, as the UNRRA men were told repeatedly when they came to Cham. Abie was dispatched to Munich to tell anyone who would listen of the importance of the festival and, above all, to urge sending the matzoh, the unleavened bread of the freed slaves snatched from certain death in the nick of time.

How well I remember that first Passover: the excitement of planning our first seder, the reading of the Exodus story of deliverance from Egyptian captivity, which this year was also our story—this Passover with hundreds of strangers who were not strangers at all, each one's story being but a variation of everyone's story. It was like no other Passover before or after. Nature itself seemed part of the festive anticipation. Storks were returning to the nests on tall chimneys they had abandoned in autumn. Delicate green buds appeared on trees, suddenly the songs of birds were heard, and fragile white flowers could be seen half hidden on the hillsides. The matzoh, however, was nowhere in sight, causing us great anxiety.

One day a truck arrived, but instead of neatly packaged American matzoh the truck was filled with bundles of used clothing: dresses, sweaters, suits, shirts, shoes, all quite worn and none too clean. These were unloaded at the camp office. Our Passover gift from America did not include even one new pair of nylons for the women. We were not grateful. Our rich American cousins had shamed us with their gift of cast-off clothing.

It was a painful lesson, yet one we needed to learn this Passover. We might not be wanderers from the desert, but we were as homeless as they had been once they left Egypt. Destitute sojourners, we too were wandering in the desert that was called Germany, despised by some just as our forebears had been, and not all that different from the runaway slaves of ancient times. But God had wrought miracles then, sending plagues and frogs upon the Egyptians, whereas no such timely misfortune had befallen the Germans. God had even parted the Red Sea for the Israelites so that all could escape. Of course we were only a remnant of a people, *She'arit Haplita,* as we were called in Hebrew, that is, a remnant of what had once been a people. I pondered these lessons of history, their differences and similarities, but was not at all sure that we would go to a Promised Land as did our once-enslaved forebears.

When it became clear that we in Cham had been forgotten, that no matzoh would reach our small camp this Passover, it was decided in mid-April that we would bake our own unleavened bread. A German bakery was requisitioned, a tiny place of no more than two rooms in one of which the oven was rendered ritually clean. UNRRA, after much excited coaxing and pleading from Abie, helped purchase sacks of flour in the surrounding area, and the entire camp population was organized into shifts of dough mixers and matzoh rollers. We were fortunate to have an experienced baker in the camp—the proud father of newborn twin boys, whose birth was considered an almost miraculous event. He taught the men how to prepare the dough and the women how to roll it out.

Matzoh baking calls for speed, above all; the dough has to be mixed rapidly lest it begin to rise. Each handful has to be rolled out quickly without being turned over; then, just as quickly, the bakers have to shove the matzoh into the oven and remove it before it burns. The bakery was small, the crowd of matzoh rollers large. We were forever getting in one another's way with our long and short (but ritually purified) rolling pins on loan from German housewives. It was hard work. It was joyous work. Men mixed. Women rolled. Everyone shouted, "Faster!" We produced matzoh that were square, round, oval, triangular, or just shapeless.

Never was the bread of freedom sweeter-tasting, nor a seder, the ritual meal eaten at the festival's start, more meaningful. When the reader of the Exodus story intoned *"Avadim hayinu"* (Slaves we were), everyone in the camp dining room knew the meaning of the words. Never again would we be slaves. But thoughts of what had been were hard to banish, and as in the years since, I couldn't help but recall our last Passover in Sosnowice when Father was still alive and when we didn't have a seder.

Although we were not aware of it at the time, that Passover was a turning point for my friends and me, and perhaps others as well. We had to begin our own exodus. To leave the camps, Germany, this meaningless, drifting existence, had to become our major goal. Greater efforts had to be made to start living. It was not, as Americans liked to put it later, a question of rebuilding our lives—most of us were too young to have ever had a life. Rather it was to build one from scratch, from the beginning. For some it meant getting married, it didn't much matter to whom, only not to be alone; others started "going" with someone in order to get married. In fact, it seemed as if we had a wedding almost every week. No one complained; the entire camp celebrated marriages, at which we were treated to festive dinners. Apparently I gave the marriage fever some thought, for on May 10, 1946, I wrote in my diary: "I don't know that I want to get married, I don't want to lose my freedom. . . ." I must have meant primarily my freedom to study, to learn, to decide on a profession, because two days later I confessed my quandary over which profession to choose.

These questions of marriage or study and career may also have arisen because that spring I fell madly in love with Gaby, a distant relative on the Padawer side, whose family had emigrated to America before the outbreak of war. By coincidence, Gaby, who was stationed in Munich, turned up in Cham one day driving a jeep. To be visited by an American soldier who was, moreover, a relative, no matter how remote, was an impressive event in our otherwise unimpressive existence. Gaby was not especially good-looking, yet he seemed everything our boys weren't. He was well groomed, had impeccable table manners, was well read, made intelligent conversation, was a good listener, and was concerned about me and "Uncle," Mother's new husband. Unfortunately, he treated me like a younger, somewhat backward sister, whereas I wanted to be taken seriously. Despite the many photographs Gaby took of me and others took of us, the romance never got off the ground. Gaby, I eventually learned, was engaged to be married, and one day he was gone. In the diary there is only one brief entry: "Everything is finished with Gaby."

To compensate for the quiet but dull life in Cham we made frequent excursions to Munich, where we saw American movies and ate ice cream, still a rare delicacy for us. Sister and I collected a small crowd of old and new acquaintances there, mostly young men at loose ends, drifting and waiting. We talked of the present and the future and rarely touched on the past, except when it reminded us of something in the present. To us the docile young people who remained in the camps of Feldafing or Landsberg were utterly ridiculous. Learning a trade, we scoffed, sitting day in, day out at sewing machines, or learning to hammer nails into wood—was that the reason we survived, were alive now? And those so-called newspapers they published in the camps! Who cared about this or that distinguished American visitor who came, looked around, and left while nothing changed! Nor did we think much of the lauded and almost at once forgotten conference of liberated Jews in January 1946, where lofty words and high-minded speeches with little connection to our daily lives and our hopes were uttered. We listened to the glib emissaries from Palestine with their promises of a carefree kibbutz life, one for all and all for one, with kibbutzniks happily dancing the hora around a bright fire. We were skeptical. It sounded too good— and, strangely, not a single one of the emissaries ever talked about study, learning, making up for years lost, when this was so much on my mind and some of my friends' minds as well. How would we ever catch up? To me, Eretz Israel increasingly seemed to be made up of kibbutz kitchens, where I would be told to peel potatoes until the end of my days. And so we young people laughed a lot and made fun of those self-important men who thought they could tell us what to do with our newfound lives. Then we went to eat another ice cream.

Like my Frankfurt friends the previous year, in Cham Ludwik Drattner showed me new possibilities. He had been beaten in the concentration camps and his bones had never mended properly, and so his body was crooked. He also had one lame leg and several missing fingernails. He was Hungarian, twenty-seven years old. Elzbieta, the camp secretary, worried that he was too old for me. But I was not "going" with Ludwik; he was simply good company for what I then considered serious conversation. Ludwik, dragging his lame leg, and I wandered in the hills around Cham, admiring the profusion of flowers and trees, watching colorful butterflies, and listening to the birds calling to one another. Bushy-tailed squirrels ran across our path and swiftly disappeared into the foliage of tall trees. We sat on a bench in the warm sunshine and looked at peaceful Cham below with its neat houses and gardens and wondered what we were doing here, why we were here in the first place. Had Ludwik been a little less crooked or a little less lame, I might have been flattered by the attention of an older man in this romantic setting. But romance was not on my mind. Nor apparently was it on Ludwik's. Poetry and literature preoccupied me then—the power of words to evoke mysterious emotions. It probably was Ludwik with his fine sense of humor who introduced me to satirical poetry. Of the two poems that I still have, one, "Two Knights," by the great German-Jewish poet Heinrich Heine, ridicules Polish patriotism together with notions of nationalism. The other, "To the Nuremberg Judges," by the Polish poet Karol Szpalski, is a scathing indictment of the Nazi trial then taking place:

Lord Judges, at leisure and with moderation
it's over and done with, it's after the war.
What's sudden can spoil, let others go hurry
but not those who judge, and not those who're guilty.
That once children were grabbed by their ankles,
their heads crushed on trees? Mere trifles, mere trifles.
That once there were people like shadows

dying of thirst? Mere memory's remembrance.
That once there were hangings, bones broken,
men grabbed and caught? It's past, long ago.
Selections for graves and deadly searches
and women's hair. Mere details for quibbling.
Captives and Pawiak, Majdanek and Auschwitz,
it's time to erase them from memory's recollecting.
That once there was typhus, gnats, lice, and darkness,
too bad, my Lords, be sparing.
Reasonable it is you're judging at leisure.
It's over and done with, it's after the war.

Roaming up and down the green hills (which surely must have been difficult for Ludwik, though he never complained), I came to understand a little why I thought the posturing of the Americans and Jews who came to see us was as absurd as that of Crapülinski and Waschlapski in Heine's poem. I also gradually realized that I was not prepared to sacrifice myself for an idea. Indeed, neither the ideas of communism, which had seemed so attractive the previous year, nor those of Zionism were sufficient cause to lay down my hard-won life for. Many years later, when I mentioned this to my teacher, Ch'en Shou-yi, at Pomona Collge, he said it reminded him of the fifth-century Chinese neo-Daoists who considered being live rebels more useful than being dead martyrs. Above idyllic Cham with its Nazi past, Ludwik and I read Polish and Yiddish and even German poetry, including the wonderful nonsense poems by Christian Morgenstern, which in their own way made much sense to me.

There was so much to learn, so much to discover. For a time I wanted to study medicine, but I had too many questions about literature, about poetry, about history, and why I lived when others died. I knew then that I would never find answers in a kibbutz kitchen. Yet I also believed that I had duties, an obligation, a debt to pay for being alive. There were reasons for still being here, my Frankfurt friends had argued, although we might never understand them. I thought for a time that if there were reasons they would be discovered or realized only in that land of Father's song, "Zion in the green fields where lambs pasture." On the other hand, the green fields of Zion were different from a kibbutz kitchen. According to my diary from those weeks of pondering choices, the Palestine option was an important one. On October 31, 1946, I wrote:

> We must have Palestine. After all, that small remnant of Jews cannot again drag itself through the world to be subjected to anti-Semitism of the nations. Jews should fight like one person with all the means at their disposal so that Palestine will be ours. But we are all selfish materialists. Everyone has another excuse for not going to Palestine. Including me. I am ashamed.

Therefore, although ashamed, even disgusted with myself for also shirking my more immediate obligations toward Mother and Sister, whom I felt I should not abandon (believing that my leaving was again a kind of abandonment), I made up my mind to go to America at the first opportunity. It was to be temporary, I vowed. After I studied, I would pay my debt. I don't know why I felt so certain that I would be able to study in America; I just knew it without anyone's having told me. Did I ask Mother's permission? Probably not. The selfish urge to live at all costs that had made me leave the family once before also drove me this time. It was not a life-or-death decision now as it had been then, but it was a fateful decision nonetheless. I often felt guilty those days— not guilty for surviving, but rather for going my own way, guilty about this grasping selfishness I couldn't, or didn't want to, con-

trol. And let it be said, Mother somehow understood that. As in
Dębica, when Mother helped me to escape, helped me to live, now
she helped arrange the journey to America. Quite unexpectedly—
and I don't know how Mother accomplished it—I was able to join
a children's transport, hoping that this time Father, had he been
alive, would have given me his approval.

The first stop for Jewish emigrants of all ages on the way to
America was the Munich Funkkaserne, several rows of two-story
German army barracks, used now as an emigration camp. American soldiers managed this camp, but perhaps nothing functioned
as they thought it should because no one understood English; the
soldiers were usually to be heard shouting at someone as though
the person were deaf. It was an incredibly dirty, barren place,
muddy in the autumn rain. Despite the fierce November cold the
barracks were not heated. The nine or ten beds in each room had
thin sacks of straw for mattresses, no sheets, and one thin, foul-
smelling blanket each. Food was minimal: one lukewarm meal a
day, mainly undercooked, sticky spaghetti with something resem-
bling tomato sauce. I shall always remember the Funkkaserne in
colors of gray—gray clouds, gray buildings, gray earth; some days
even the tomato sauce seemed to have a gray tinge.

The children's transport (the "children" were all older than I)
represented only a tiny fraction of those waiting to be shipped
out. Most of the emigrants in the Funkkaserne were Jewish
adults. However, among the camp population were also non-Jews,
mostly Ukrainians, so it seemed, sponsored by their American
relatives. Jews and Ukrainians did not get along, the former sus-
pecting the latter of having been camp guards, and the Ukrainians having yet to shed their traditional anti-Semitism. Many of
the Ukrainians were camp managers and, as block elders, were

trusted by the Americans. Part of their function was to distribute CARE packages to the camp population, and they used it to excellent advantage by removing the three most coveted black market items: cigarettes, chocolate, and coffee. I was gaining a new perspective on Americans; when in authority they seemed less like supermen and more like ill-tempered, ignorant men. Why could they not learn to tell a Jew from a non-Jew and a thief from an honest person, we asked one another.

I was in the Funkkaserne for only six weeks, yet it seemed much longer, conditions being what they were. Things were made worse by an incident that occurred after about two weeks. Seven other girls and I, unable to wash in the unsegregated, cold-water wash-rooms and unable to heat the room in which we were staying because we had only large wet logs with neither kindling nor paper, decided one evening to transform the one empty bed into fire-wood. We soon had a blazing fire. We washed for the first time since arriving, even did laundry; then suddenly a Ukrainian block elder burst into the room (he had probably seen the smoke from our chimney) shouting what we thought were obscenities since none of us understood Ukrainian. The next day, like prisoners, albeit clean ones, we were marched to the Americans' office, where, predictably, a red-faced soldier shouted at us. Since we did not understand English, we could only surmise that he was angry. But so, for that matter, were we. Didn't the Ukrainians steal our choco-late? And why weren't we given usable firewood? We said this to the American in Yiddish, Polish, and several other languages, which he, in turn, didn't understand. Finally an interpreter informed us that we had sabotaged American property and would be deprived of our American visas. Later the sentence was commuted to con-finement to camp, which did not trouble me, since I knew that all fences have holes, can be climbed over, or can be dug under.

In years thereafter I often pondered the meaning of this trivial incident and why it left so strong an imprint. Did it represent the intriguing game of power, to curry favor by means of denunciation, a practice well known from ghettos and camps? Or was it also an attempt to remind the victim of his victimhood? Whatever it was that motivated the Ukrainian to denounce and the American to punish, I realized that I needn't feel like a victim if I chose not to. It was a question of choices one could make, or not make.

From the Funkkaserne our children's transport was moved to another emigration camp in Bremen, which, compared with Munich, had luxury accommodations, in what may have been a school dormitory. These camps were apparently conceived along the line of holding pens where, instead of cattle, human cargo was held in readiness to board a ship as soon as one became available. It was, no doubt, an efficient method, though rather lacking in human consideration. Despondent and alone—we eight girls from the Funkkaserne having been dispersed among the Bremen camp population—I observed my seventeenth birthday there.

I began to have qualms about leaving, although, according to my diary, I tried to assure myself that I was making this journey in order to study. All my acquaintances were sailing one by one, and on January 19, 1947, I lamented the emptiness of the dormitory. A week later, after having boarded the *Marine Perch,* I wrote how really absurd it was to be traveling alone into the world. The entry for January 28 is the last one, and it notes sadly how much I longed for my mother.

From an unfinished letter written on board ship, but apparently never sent:

Here are the first impressions of the ship, as I have never seen one before. The *Marine Perch* is not very large. However, one always gets lost. I run around for hours on end until I find our cabin, the toilets. . . . The ocean is enormously impressive. You cannot imagine

how beautiful it is. Although we are still only in the [English] Chan-
nel, I am totally taken by it. You can stare into the water for hours
and think of the most wonderful things.

There are three decks, like a building of three storys. The third
and second are very nice, as are the toilets, washrooms, and cabins
there, which are smaller and airier. E deck [where I was] is terrible;
toilets have no doors, there are more than thirty people in each
cabin, there are no windows, only ventilators. It is extremely hot.

The food is wonderful. But the people's behavior is abominable. I
blush with shame. They don't just eat, they devour their food and, to
eat even faster and more, they eat with their hands.

[Five days later.] Stormy weather for many days now. The ship is
tossed about like a nutshell. I can no longer go on deck; after five
minutes I am soaking wet. Everyone is terribly seasick and no one
cares what he looks like any longer. Men are growing beards, women
run around half dressed (provided they can run). I am not seasick
and every day I go to eat in the empty dining room, where I am
served by three stewards. In my and others' estimation I am indeed
very brave.

The ship sprang a hole, but the stewards say it isn't dangerous.

The weather is miserable. Stormy every day.

The ship did not sink. The storms ceased. And one day I
arrived in New York. It was another way station where I knew I
would not remain long.

After less than two years I moved to Los Angeles, to which
Mother and her husband came two years later, in 1950. She
looked wonderful, her hair nicely cut and waved, the haunted
look gone. No one would have suspected that only six years earlier
this elegant lady stood in the cold slush of Birkenau, emaciated
and uncertain as to whether she and her daughter would live to
see the next day. Sister arrived two years after that. She too looked
well and was even more beautiful than when I had last seen her.

In Los Angeles in the nineteen-fifties most people seemed to be from elsewhere. Having left their pasts in the places they came from, they lived in the present. And so did we for a time, like true Californians. Gradually we became a family—albeit a new family, unlike the old one, in a new place. Both Sister and I married, had children. I studied Chinese, beginning a new journey, a journey of the mind, which took me far away from Mielec and from Poland. We celebrated birthdays and holidays, had Jewish friends, and spoke only English. It made for minimal communication at first, which was just as well. We wanted to be American, talk about now, and maybe go to Canter's Deli on Fairfax Avenue to eat bagels with cream cheese and lox. Mother cooked wonderful dinners and baked elegant cakes, and, like in the fairy tale, I want to write now that we lived happily ever after. But we didn't.

That was not because we suffered special hardships or encountered insurmountable problems. No, we led quite ordinary lives in the ever-expanding suburbia of Los Angeles and had our small joys and petty annoyances. Without being aware of it, we learned to appear in daily life as someone other than who we were, and we congratulated ourselves for how well we played the role. "You must be from England," people would say to me, "from Australia maybe." I was pleased; no one except close friends should know that I was "dancing at other people's weddings," as Hanna Krall wrote in a short story of the same title. It was important to conceal from others our anxieties, compulsive behavior, strange phobias, fears, and nightmares, and the physical maladies such as various intestinal disorders, undiagnosable aches, and fatigue. More difficult to hide were skewed emotional reactions to certain situations, when we laughed instead of crying, or reacted stonily when an emotional response was called for. There were the strange sensitivities, the offhand remarks that caused people to give us an odd look followed by the long silence we had come to dread. But all these appeared later, long after we thought that our "new lives" had begun. They took still more years to recognize for what they were.

There were many kinds of anxieties. Mine centered around sickness, doctors, and hospitals. Every illness was dangerous: children's stuffy noses, stomach pains, bloody elbows or knees, were all equally frightening, for they could lead to unthinkable complications. Doctors were not to be trusted, especially those who refused to give detailed explanations. Who knew what they were hiding? It might be something terrible about my child's condition they didn't want me to know. More than once a doctor showed me the door, telling me never to come again with my sick children. Hospitals were to be avoided at all costs. Didn't I know that those who went in never came out? The constant threat of loss always hovered just over the horizon. And since I knew how precarious all existence really was, I had to be constantly vigilant, always prepared to protect and save my family. Ready cash had to be hidden in a safe place in case of hurried departure; food had to be on hand in case of an emergency; some gold jewelry needed to be readily accessible. Experience had taught me that gold could always be traded for necessities. One day I realized, however, that my fears and anxieties were like unwelcome companions on a journey. Though they were heartily disliked, we were doomed to move through life together.

Eventually the Los Angeles way station too had to be left behind. With my completion of a doctorate in Chinese history, another journey had to begin. The journey to Jerusalem may have been the result of a debt incurred many years before that I thought needed redeeming. Or was it, after all, Father's song of Zion that led me to this, yet another way station?

CHAPTER SEVEN

══════════

IN THE BEGINNING

The white mountain swans, who dwell on the pure, heavenly moun-
tain lake, must leave the lake one day. They must travel far and wide,
from one mud puddle to another mud puddle. Once their journeys
are done, the white swans again return to their blue mountain lake.

A Buddhist parable

The deportation action of 1938 became a paradigm for later
National Socialist actions against Jews: It was the first large-scale
deportation requiring coordination between the police, the Reichs-
bahn railway, diplomats, and financial authorities.

TRUDE MAURER, "The Background for Kristallnacht:
The Expulsion of Polish Jews"

I began this story with the end of Jewish Mielec. But this is not
where the story of the end begins. Maybe I should have started
with a history of Mielec, the town's origin and its development
into a fairly important market town, and the growth of its Jewish
population. But what is the aim of my enterprise? Am I writing
the history of Jewish Mielec? Or can I do no more than write the
stories meant to inform history, those stories which may (or may
not) become history? Even in telling what I can of Jewish Mielec
and its end, I know that this too is a mere fragment, and only my
version of its end. There are other versions, including a version

captured in photographs, which show men, women, and children whose anguished faces betray their fear of an unknown fate. Therefore, let me begin here with yet another fragment, with the people, the family.

I know next to nothing about my maternal grandparents. They were long dead when I was born. Presumably they, or their parents, came from Russia to Leipzig, in German Saxony, a town of wealthy merchants and fairs. I don't know the exact dates of birth of Fanny and Moses Ganger, my mother's parents, except that Fanny died in 1914 and Moses followed her one year later. Between 1892 and 1903 the couple had eleven children, three sons and eight daughters.

My mother, who had a remarkable memory and knew many details about relatives and their relatives' relatives, never said much about her parents or her childhood, even though, born in 1901, she was already thirteen years old when her mother died. Was it because, sandwiched between five older and two younger sisters, she did not have the happiest childhood? All I know is that Fanny and Moses had a food store where, my mother once mentioned, they sold fresh cheese. My imagination, probably not altogether inaccurately, has filled the store with—in addition to cheeses—jars of dried beans, sugar, and hard candy, and barrels of pickles and sauerkraut.

My grandparents may have been a good-looking couple: Their daughters had even features and several were quite pretty. A distinguishing attribute of the Ganger sisters was their well-formed, small nose; like small feet, such a nose was considered an asset in girls. A photograph that has mysteriously survived the ravages of time and war shows the eight sisters in 1917, arranged according to age. They are wearing sensible dresses or blouses, devoid of any frills or laces. None of them wears any jewelry, except for the next-to-youngest, who has earrings. My aunt Rosa, the oldest, was only twenty-three years old at the time, yet with her pince-nez and double chin she already looks like an elderly lady. It was she who presumably took charge of her younger sisters after their mother died. She is a commanding presence in the photograph and must have been so in real life. She wouldn't have endeared herself to the two youngest ones, aged fifteen and fourteen in 1917. The older of the two looks at me defiantly, while the youngest girl, my aunt Friedel, is sullen, with not a hint of a smile. No wonder she escaped early from under Rosa's stern rule and joined the Communist Party, where she met Arno. In the photograph, the face of my mother, Helene, is somewhat crooked and swollen—an abscessed wisdom tooth, she said, when I once asked. No similar picture exists for the boys. In fact, aside from this photograph, there is no other memento of that generation of my family, except Moses's solid-gold pocket watch. It is still in working order today, continuing my grandfather's time.

In contrast to the Leipzig relatives, Father's family, the Geminders, were small-town, shtetl Jews. Although Mielec was a market town to which villagers came from the surrounding area to sell produce and buy necessities, it could not compare with Leipzig, with its wealthy merchants and its fairs. The reason I know so much more about this unimportant Galician town and the Geminder family may have to do with the stories Father was fond of telling. Or perhaps I remember them from long ago, when the women congregated on an afternoon in Grandmother Mindel's kitchen and told stories to which Esther and I listened.

In the beginning was Great-grandmother Blime, who had three husbands, a relative once told me. How old Blime was at any point while she was marrying and burying husbands is not known, since the only definite date is 1859, when a son by her second husband was born. When her second husband died, she was obviously still young enough to marry a third time and give birth to her second son, Hayim, my grandfather. Blime was alive when World War I broke out and she died at the ripe old age of ninety-nine, my cousin Eva told me.

Blime's third husband, my great-grandfather Israel Geminder, was a widower whose daughter, Rivke, whom he had brought with him into the marriage, later belonged to the Geminder family of the Small Market. Israel was a peddler, making the rounds of villages on foot to take orders for goods from Polish and Jewish peasants and deliver the items ordered. He would have been gone the greater part of the week, returning only to purchase the goods ordered and to prepare for the Sabbath. I don't know when he died—it was before World War I—but Blime outlived him by many years. Being a widower, he was perhaps older than his wife. Blime, who wore that white turban with the three strands of pearls, commanded the respect even of Grandmother Mindel, her daughter-in-law, who was not known for respecting others. It was Mindel who had arranged a small room for the aged Blime next to the store, where her presence still seemed to linger many years after she had passed away.

Hayim, my grandfather, married Mindel, who was from Dębica, and the couple prospered. They had three children: the two girls, Feige and Sheindl, and my father, Yedidia, who was born in 1891. Unlike his father, Grandfather Hayim no longer walked the villages on foot. He had acquired a horse and wagon, and he was able to visit more villages, cover greater distances, and carry more (probably also larger and heavier) goods. For the most part peasants bought small items: ribbons for tying up braids; combs and hand mirrors for brides; thread and needles; cloth for skirts and blouses; buttons; woolen shawls; new boots from the shoemaker. But by the time Grandfather Hayim acquired his horse and wagon, a thriving feather industry had sprung up in Mielec, managed mostly by the town's Jews. He was probably one of sev-

eral wagoners who bought up feathers in the villages for sale
to the Mielec "industrialists" who manufactured featherbedding.
Precisely when this enterprise appeared is uncertain; it was not yet
in evidence in 1891. His career as a wagoner may have begun with
carrying grain, for there were as many as six grain dealers in
Mielec's Jewish community.

Whether because he had made money as a wagoner, or because
of some shady business deal (as a relative hinted without di-
vulging more detail), when wealthy Mielec families began to
erect stone houses, Hayim abandoned the peripatetic life. He built
that fine two-story house on the newly developed Sandomierska
Street, behind the Large Market. As I've said, the store was on the
ground floor, three rooms were above it, and above those was an
attic where chickens and geese suffered miserably on market day.
This would have been in the first decade of the twentieth century,
after the great fire in 1900, which consumed many of Mielec's
wooden structures. The store advertised itself on a 1911 postcard
as a specialty store of chocolates and "southern fruits," perhaps
bananas and oranges, maybe lemons. But that was in the good old
days, before World War I. By the nineteen-thirties those luxuries
had given way to more mundane necessities, like herring, pickles,
and flour. As I also said earlier, the house, nearly unchanged,
except for a stone staircase rather than a wooden one to the second floor, was still standing at Sandomierska 15 (now called
Mickiewicza) when I visited Mielec in 1980.

Growing up in Mielec, which is in western Galicia, differed
greatly from growing up in Leipzig. While my mother went to a
secular German school, my father attended one of the communal
heder schools, where Jewish boys from the age of three or four
were initiated into the Bible, commentaries, and prayers. His sisters no doubt remained at home, learning the prayers, the Hebrew
alphabet, and how to do sums from their mother, Mindel, who

capably managed the store's finances and prayed devoutly every Sabbath wearing her fashionable gray wig. The children would have also learned to read books in Yiddish. These had gradually begun to appear in Poland's small towns, to the delight of the unruly heder boys, young Yedidia, I imagine, among them.

Traveling booksellers, their handcarts piled high with reading matter, made the rounds of small Galician towns. The books they sold—mostly German-language, I was told—were not religious books, but for the greater part on secular topics. Those boys who sensed a world out there beyond the confines of their small town were not above stealing coins wherever they could to buy the books. Despite their parents' and their teachers' vigilance, they would manage to waylay the bookseller and, clutching their treasures, find an unused or little-frequented attic. There they taught themselves the Latin alphabet (not impossible with a knowledge of Yiddish) and started reading "forbidden" matter. These "wild ones," as they were called, were usually caught, punishment was meted out, and life would return to its accustomed ways . . . until the next visit from the bookseller. Meanwhile, however, by means of these books a number of boys, my father among them, were learning to read languages other than Hebrew.

Aside from the bookseller, the World War I adventures of Mindel and Blime, who by then must have been well over sixty years old, also had a place in family lore. Mielec and some of the surrounding villages were strategically located on the Wisłoka River. By mid-September 1914, the area had become a battleground for the advancing Russian and defending Austrian armies; when Mielec seemed doomed, many of the townspeople, including Blime and Mindel, decided to flee. Here there is a gap in the story. Did Feige and Sheindl remain behind, or did they flee? Father, we know, had been sent to Holland earlier, dispatched there by Grandmother Mindel to avoid his being drafted into the Austrian army. Whatever the case, the two women went to Vienna, where they expected to find shelter with Mindel's supplier of chocolates. Traveling by train—itself a novelty for these small-town women—was accomplished without a mishap.

But as soon as they arrived in Vienna their troubles began. They may have become confused by the hustle and bustle, the confusion of broad and narrow streets, the tall buildings; neither of the women had ever been in this large a city. Or perhaps they were exhausted and disoriented from the long journey. Whatever the reason, at some point Mindel lost Blime and panicked—though it may have been Blime who lost Mindel. Maybe Blime became curious about the well-dressed ladies in their fashionable hats and furs and, distracted by the many carriages, simply wandered off, only to find suddenly that she was lost. Mother and daughter-in-law were, of course, eventually reunited, but the story of the search, and Mindel's panic and adventures, was told and retold with much relish and many a new embellishment. The women must have remained in Vienna (with or without the chocolate supplier's help) for nearly eight months, as battles in the Mielec area continued throughout the winter and spring of 1915. But where they lived and how they supported themselves were never mentioned. It was the story of how they lost and found each other that mattered.

Blime and Mindel soon returned home. But my father did not. For the next twenty-four years he made his home elsewhere, thinking perhaps that he had left the shtetl behind for good. It wasn't that he hated or despised Mielec; to the contrary. Yet neither did he expect in all those years, I believe, to be thrust back into it after he had lost everything he had worked for over nearly a quarter of a century.

There is no record of when and where my parents were married, how long they had known each other, or whether they had fallen in love. It might have been that my mother, having attended secretarial school and being considered a "professional" woman, met and became attracted to this fun-loving man who liked music and theater. Or maybe it was an arranged match. According to one version, Dora, one of my aunts living in Holland then, was the matchmaker. She had befriended the young man from Poland, who, to all appearances, had shed the vestiges of his shtetl past. In a photograph (now lost), taken in 1917 or 1918, when he was twenty-six or twenty-seven years old, Father wore a well-cut suit, complete with vest and fashionable panama hat, and he was leaning on his cane and smiling happily into the camera. According to another version, it was Mother's oldest sister, Rosa, who arranged the match. She had married into Father's family and her husband knew the bachelor from Poland who should have been married long ago.

My parents must have been married around 1922. The wedding may have been in Leipzig, where most of the sisters lived; or perhaps they were married in Holland, where Dora would have seen to a proper wedding. That it was an elegant and highly respectable affair was obvious from their now long-lost wedding picture, which, like my father's photograph in Holland, I often looked at as a child. My mother, in a white wedding dress and a veil that was pinned back at her ears, was seated, while slightly behind her and to her side stood my father in elegant frock coat, with a top hat in the crook of his arm. She looked apprehensive, indeed outright frightened, whereas he smiled gleefully, almost triumphantly, even though an orphan was not considered a desirable catch. According to Grandmother Mindel, Mother was also slightly taller than her husband, which in a wife was highly undesirable.

After Yedidia and Helene were married, they went to live in Halle, Germany, on the Saale River. Both my sister Lore and I were born there. Halle had not been as hospitable to Jews as Leipzig, alternately persecuting and expelling them, and its Jewish community in 1920 numbered less than two thousand. By 1933, the number had declined to around one thousand. Yet Halle, hardly a backwater, also had something to recommend it. The city had a considerable number of commercial and manufacturing enterprises and an active printing and publishing industry. Its university, founded near the end of the seventeenth century, was recognized after 1815 as a major center of learning for Protestant theology. More to the point was the fact that relatives from both my parents' sides of the family had come to live in Halle, including my father's sister Sheindl and her husband.

Establishing themselves in the city after Germany's defeat in World War I took my parents years. At first they lived modestly in a small apartment, even after my sister and I were born. But whether my father had to borrow money (if so, most likely it was from Mother's relatives), or whether he had saved up capital while in Holland, by 1930 he had acquired a fairly substantial store on one of Halle's major thoroughfares. In the spacious shop he sold an assortment of small items: stockings, baby clothes, lingerie, yarns and wools of all kinds, and lace handkerchiefs, the delicate laces of which my mother crocheted. Despite Germany's postwar economic difficulties, business must have been good. I have a photograph taken during those Weimar Republic years, dating perhaps from 1927 or 1928. The sisters Hanna, Rosa, and my mother are grouped in a semicircle with Uncle Leo, Hanna's husband. My sister Lore, a child of four or five, stands in front of them. The three women are wearing fashionable dresses and low-heeled shoes (they tended to be as tall as or taller than their husbands). The photograph must have been taken in summer, for the women and the child wear short-sleeved dresses. Father, who was known to be addicted to photography, may have been the photographer; or perhaps it was Rosa's husband, whose cane Hanna is holding.

My first memories, from around the age of three, are of a large five-room flat in a well-kept building on a street lined with chestnut trees. Although this flat was home, I soon became aware that home was also elsewhere. For the first six or seven years of my life the family's existence turned on two pivots: Halle and Mielec, my father's home. In Halle all was order: neat and clean and predictable; meals served on time; the orderly disorder of family visits, birthdays, and holidays, when aunts and uncles, even the Leipzig relatives, congregated in one or another home. In Mielec, nothing was predictable. Visitors dropped in at any time of day; nothing was ever quite clean, either in the store or in the upstairs apartment; water was bought by the bucket in the street; fires were lit with wood kindling. I was attracted to the differences as a child, to their smells (not all of them pleasant) and their sounds. I remember the smell of Grandmother's chicken soup cooking, and the chants and haunting melodies I heard from the rebbe's house across the street on Friday evenings, as well as the tall dark men with long black beards and black coats I saw when we visited Mielec.

Even in Halle the Mielec family was not kept remote. Their unseen presence was discussed at mealtimes, and invariably for Hanukkah a large package of Grandmother Mindel's *non,* a dark brown, sticky honey-and-nut concoction only she knew how to make, arrived. As I grew up, I thought of Mielec as both familiar and strange, both nearby and far; it belonged to my father and therefore also, in some way, to me. Or I to it.

I am about to unpack memories, as literary scholar Stephen Owen has it, attempting to write about the half-remembered and the never-to-be-remembered. No one can corroborate my memories. Neither Mother nor any of her sisters is alive, and long ago I lost contact with their children, my cousins, who were either killed or scattered to the four corners of the earth. "A memory is a broken shard of the past," writes Owen, and that is indeed all I have, a few shards. To make a story from these excavated, unpacked shards, once part of a whole, is not easy.

In my earliest recollected awareness of myself I am standing in the kitchen of our apartment and looking at a shaft of sunlight pouring in through the half-open window. Specks of dust are dancing in the light. I try to get hold of them, opening my hand, grabbing, and closing tightly. But each time, I find nothing in my open hand. Each time my hand is as empty as it was before. It is a mystery—something that is nothing, nothing that is nonetheless something.

There would be other such mysteries later: earthworms that appeared silently on the surface of the earth and vanished in a flash. Where to? Ants that had no eyes, yet could march one after the other without ever straying from the long column. Flies that did not avoid the sticky flypaper, but instead suicidally attached themselves to it. Inanimate things were differently but equally mysterious. They didn't vanish as if they had never been, nor were they something that turned out to be nothing. Inanimate things had a tendency to come apart, change shape. Unlike silent earthworms, inanimate things changed shape noisily, and this brought scolding adults onto the scene.

My small world was the spacious flat and its high windows, which overlooked the street in front and the courtyard with its large lilac tree in back. The living room was meant to be lived in. In it stood the long dining table, my father's desk, his radio, and an imposing sideboard of dark brown wood on which my mother's precious crystal vases and bowls were arranged on delicate doilies. My sister and I each had our own room. I sometimes played in mine but preferred the large bathroom that had a tub, a storage wardrobe, and my father's shaving table. My toys were stored next to the shaving table in the kind of basket women carried on their backs.

In this small world, Frieda, who was a professional housekeeper-nursemaid my family employed, was the supreme ruler. My world also included my father's store, where Frieda might take me when she had errands to run. There, my father ruled. Strangely, in both the flat and the store, Mother was assigned, and perhaps gladly assumed, a secondary role. That is, until one day Frieda, weeping bitterly, was forced to depart because Jews were no longer allowed to have German help.

Frieda was a small, gray-haired woman never seen without her large white apron. She had blue eyes that looked sternly at her domain from behind sparkling rimless glasses. Her long skinny braid was coiled into a tight knot at the back of her head. In the afternoons, she always smelled of lemon, because, her work done, she rubbed her hands with lemon rinds, considering these better than hand cream. Frieda was not from Halle. She had never married and she seemed to have no family. I think she had been with one or another of my mother's sisters as their children were growing up. We were the last of the line.

My parents were totally dependent on Frieda. I loved her, but my sister Lore hated her. Frieda taught me many things, including how to recognize the waxing and waning of the moon. She was the one who punished me for misdeeds, made me eat Cream of Wheat, which I detested, and enforced proper behavior. Having no other home, she was always there, day in, day out. Holidays meant my parents could be charmed and manipulated. But Frieda, who was home day after day, could not be swayed to relax rules. For my parents she ran a tidy household on a strictly predictable schedule. She firmly believed that Lore's conduct needed supervising, and established rules and regulations for her. There is no denying that she was a tyrant who believed in discipline and obedience from children. But there is also no denying that she had a mind of her own at a time when independent thinking was not exactly in vogue in Germany. She was said to have declared in 1933, when Hitler came to power, that she did not need a leader (*Führer*). Her outspokenness in expressing her contempt for the goose-stepping Nazi SA then and later must have terrified my parents.

While my parents spent the day in the store Frieda managed the household in exemplary fashion. Whenever Mother was home Frieda relinquished her hold on the kitchen. There I would spend hours, watching Mother, with a sure hand, scale fish, slice the thinnest noodles, mix sweet batter for cakes. Considerately, she never scraped the bowl entirely clean, but left some of the raw batter for me. When the family gathered at our home on festive occasions, she prepared steamed yeast dumplings, which were eaten with a rich meat sauce. (Years later, when I had my first taste of Chinese steamed bread, *mantou,* I realized with a shock of recognition that it was none other than my childhood delicacy.) The kitchen was a place of many fragrances. Mother's delicate smell—she used a special face cream—mingled with those from her pots or baking pans.

Sometimes the older nieces and nephews helped in the kitchen. Cousin Herbert, who later became a baker in Bolivia, was as a teenager already fond of cooking. Some said that he spoke to his food as it boiled and bubbled on the stove and was overheard saying to Jell-O: "Stop quivering, you'll be eaten anyway."

I don't know if Mother and I talked much in the kitchen. Sometimes she sang one of her unmelodious songs; unlike Father, she couldn't carry a tune. One song in particular had many verses about a girl who had gone to meet her lover in a myrtle grove and was then surprised by her mother, who threatens to send her to the nunnery. Frieda most certainly did not approve of such songs. But then Frieda never sang.

Both Father and Mother hovered over me when I was ill, which was frequently. They arrived at my bed with a thermometer, a large bottle of iodine—sore throats were painted with iodine—and finally with a succession of cups of chamomile tea, my mother's sure cure for every illness. They fussed a great deal over me and I remember rather liking it. They would bring me my favorite books, even on occasion those precious ones that were kept in the bookcase with the glass doors. Once, when I had whooping cough, my father prepared a foolproof Mielec remedy: the juice of a roasted beet, the hot brown syrup guaranteed to ease my cough. I seemed to take a long time recovering, but Father swore if not for the beet syrup it would have taken even longer. They even fussed over minor maladies, like bloody knees, carefully cleaning the wound and applying iodine. Wrapping the long bandage around the injured knee always required two people: one to minister to the injury, the other to quiet the screaming child with promises neither parent intended to keep. As much as I abhorred the painful sting of iodine, I will always associate it with my parents' loving ministrations. I often wonder if the soothing, nonstinging antibacterial ointment of my children's childhood can evoke similar memories.

My parents and I spent carefree times together. We took long walks along the river, and I was sometimes allowed to accompany Mother to Café Huth, where she met her sisters and sister-in-law and I was treated to a large piece of chocolate cake while listening to the women's gossip. I vividly remember a visit in Mielec, where we were received as honored guests and where I, for the first time in my short life, played in the street. According to later accounts, I was horridly misbehaved, putting Cousin Esther in a box and sitting on top of it. When I fell ill, Grandmother Mindel tried to feed me vile-smelling and even worse-tasting gruel.

The best times of all were birthdays, mine and others'. They were celebrated in grand style by the entire family on both Father's and Mother's sides. Aunts, uncles, and cousins came from Leipzig bringing large and small presents; a huge birthday dinner was prepared; and Father tirelessly played Viennese waltzes on his record player. For one birthday in particular (was it my fourth?) he had built for me a doll's store, each little drawer filled with marzipan fruit and vegetables. Its sign in Yiddish read "Blime's Store," and I was the proud owner. For that same birthday I received my first umbrella. Unfortunately, I used it to drive Aunt Friedel, who had come all the way from Frankfurt for the celebration, from the room. She never forgot.

It was a charmed childhood. No wonder Lore told me years later that she felt neglected, and ignored, because I received everyone's attention. Indeed, as the youngest on both sides of the family, and surrounded by adults, I was spoiled and protected. I neither had a need for nor did I miss playmates, being totally content with the company of my older cousins. Life was lived in a close family circle, and though my parents must have known many Jewish families, those families were not part of our daily life. After the war, Friedel, who was no less a communist than before the war, accused us, cruelly I thought, of lacking social and political consciousness. She was then, it would seem, already critical of German Jews, believing that they brought the calamities they suffered upon themselves. But this is blaming the victims for their victimization.

Surely my parents weren't oblivious to the political instability of the Weimar Republic or, when it ended, to the increasing anti-Semitism in Germany. My first awareness of sorrow and grief occurred when Frieda told me ever so gently that tall Uncle Max, the one who had lifted me high on his shoulders until I thought I could touch the heavens, was dead. Although I didn't know then what dying meant, I did realize that I would never see him again. Much later I learned that although he had believed in national socialism early on, he had come to see that no good would come of Nazi hate and Hitler's anti-Semitism, and had committed suicide in 1933.

Time passed swiftly. I turned five and then six and began to see and hear more. One day Frieda packed her large suitcase, crying bitterly as she did so, and then was gone. No doubt my sister Lore was secretly happy to be done with Frieda, but for my parents and me there was suddenly a gaping emptiness. Püppe (her real name was Friedel), Aunt Clara's orphaned eldest daughter, came to live with us. Then Aunt Bekka, my mother's older sister and Uncle Max's widow, also moved in. She took Frieda's old room, which still contained some of her lemony presence. Püppe and I did not get along. She was only a year older than Lore and formed a united front with her against me. Aside from that, not much changed, or so it seemed. My parents still went to the store in the morning, returning at midday for the main meal. Lore still went to school each day. And I, with some help from others, was teaching myself how to read.

Yet beneath the surface calm and the daily routine there was an ominous unease. New words appeared in conversations at the dinner table. "*Rishes,*" Mother said often and emphatically, speaking the Yiddish word for anti-Semitism. Palestine was frequently mentioned; Sally Kanner, Father's cousin, had gone to see for himself whether to resettle his family there. "*Hakhsharah*"—the Hebrew word for training for Palestine—said Lore, who now belonged to a Zionist youth group where she made new friends. The little blue box with the likeness of Theodor Herzl, the founder of modern Zionism, on it, which hung over the radio and into which

I put coins every Friday afternoon, assumed a new reality, connected with a real place. This was money for Palestine, for Zion, and for the green fields of Father's song. I was told under no circumstances to speak to the girl who lived with her parents in the basement; her father wore the brown SA uniform. Not that I wanted to speak to or play with her—her sharp, unsmiling face was always hostile.

I remember that customers were ever fewer in the store, and there was one disturbing incident when *Jude* was painted on the store window. This may have been at the time of the Nazi boycott in 1938 when the Geminder store too was blacklisted. Meanwhile, the shouting voices emanating from Father's radio in the living room became shriller and louder, more vicious, sinister, and threatening. I learned about war and bombs when Father read to me a newspaper account of the Spanish Civil War; he was sitting at his desk and I on his lap. Spain was remote, somewhere far off, and it seemed to me that neither bombs nor war could touch me as long as I was close to my father.

Once I started school I began to think myself quite grown up. But Lore, now a teenager, and I were no longer on sisterly terms. She grew increasingly distant and spent more time in her youth group. It would meet afternoons and there were frequent outings. I had no part in her new life and was told I was too young. How well I remember feeling left out, shunted aside for reasons that didn't seem valid. I too wanted to belong to something, some group outside of the family. Before me as I write this is an old photograph of her youth group, two boys and seven girls, all smiling delightedly from the hillock on which they are sitting. It must be autumn, for there are trees with bare branches in the background and the youngsters are wearing sweaters. I recognize Cousins Ette (Püppe's sister Senta) and Heini, who were both killed in Kołomyja. Of the five remaining, some went to England, others to Palestine. The photograph was taken more than sixty years ago, when these teenagers dreamt youthful dreams that never came true.

My going to school was not as traumatic for me as it was for my parents. I had not been anxious to start school, nor was I excited about this new turn in my life. Among several dozen girls in the class, Cousin Ruth and I were the only Jews. While she didn't seem to be a target for the animosity and taunts of our classmates, I was almost daily attacked both verbally and physically. "Jew pig," they screamed, and they ostracized me on the playground. I was not prepared to suffer these verbal assaults and would lash out, push or hit the offender. Invariably, our teacher, a Mr. Brückner, was informed, and he punished me in front of the class by slapping my face. Undaunted, I resorted to fighting my tormentors on the way home, arriving at the store after these fights disheveled, buttons torn off my coat, dirt and dead leaves in my hair. Cousin Ruth, by comparison, came home as immaculate as when she had left. When I asked her a few years ago, she remembered nothing of this. But the fact is that Ruth had a Christian friend with whom she walked back and forth to school. I suspect this girl protected her from the insults that I seemingly invited. Neither girl wanted to be seen with me, and many a fight took place between Ruth's friend and me. How sad, I think today, that these children, no doubt gentle girls most of them, were infected with their parents' terrible sickness at such an early age.

My parents were obviously upset, fearing that these childish skirmishes would have repercussions for the entire family. Mother tried to prevail on me not to retaliate. But she seemed not to understand: Yes, I was a Jew, but I was not a pig. From my childish point of view, the two simply didn't belong together. In the end, these troubles did not last very long, because I attended school for only a little over one year. And then it was October 1938.

AUGUST 1999

My son, Jonathan Michael, has a large house with a large yard in a Boston suburb. He also has a large dog. And he has a successful career in a large bank. He has grown into a kind and caring man. But I still see the small boy who was always on the move, running, with me in hot pursuit to save him from coming to harm, from the terrible dangers lurking somewhere out there—to save him from falling off the slide, the fence, the tree; from sickness, from pain; from people who might harm him. His carefree, happy childhood was for me a time of nameable and unnameable fears and terrors. When he and his sister, Miriam Alisa, turned ten and nine, the age I had been when World War II broke out, I became even more vigilant, watching for signs of their ability to survive. I wanted to make sure they would be able to endure what I had, that they would be strong when they had to be. Were they survivors? To be on the safe side, they had not been named after anyone in the family who had not survived. Although I did not realize it at the time, being a mother to my son and daughter meant above all protecting and saving them from great dangers, as my mother had once saved me.

Our family has gathered this year in my son's large house. There are eight of us: Lore and her husband, her two daughters and grandson, my son, my daughter, and me. I still have my (by now well-hidden) fears, but it is the younger generation that tries to protect me—not from dangers, for there are none, only from small inconveniences: the evening cool, a sudden shower, the hot sun. They are so normal, those young ones, and I think how incredibly strange I must have seemed to my children when they were young and when they compared me to other mothers they knew.

Lore and I are sitting in my son's backyard under a tall shade tree. The afternoon sun sends showers of sparks through the tree's dense foliage where, invisible from below, a bird is calling to its mate. The dog sleeps fitfully at our feet, its nose twitching, perhaps in dreams of a chase and food. It is peaceful here in this middle-class suburban Massachusetts neighborhood with its well-kept houses and neatly trimmed lawns. Quite incongruous with the task Lore and I have before us: we are about to fill out a sheaf of forms of many pages and many questions for a database designed to make us "retrievable" survivors at some future time. Recently, as survivors are about to become "extinct" ("They're dying out," someone wrote, and I am reminded of the hapless dinosaurs), Swiss banks have acknowledged Jewish accounts and insurance companies are admitting to unpaid claims. Multibillion-dollar concerns reluctantly remember the slave laborers who made them rich more than half a century ago. As Lore and I fill out the forms with their strange questions, we laugh and have no illusions; more than likely we'll become a footnote in someone's Ph.D. dissertation.

We have forms for insurance claims and forms for years of unpaid slave labor. Of course, we are certain that Father must have had insurance; he was a responsible businessman, a man concerned for his family's welfare should something happen to him. But how are we to know how much life insurance he may have had, or with which insurance company? This kind of information is not generally imparted to young children, or even teenagers. Parents are not in the habit of telling their offspring how much their death is worth. We have read about lists of names of unpaid claims: 160,000 names, writes one; 147,000, another; still another mentions 300,000 names, later mysteriously reduced to 100,000. Some write that the insurance companies won't allow publicizing the lists. Others write that only a few thousand names will be published. Some write that Yad Vashem, the Jerusalem Holocaust Memorial, has the lists, or will have them, but has promised not to make them public. I have made telephone calls to inquire about the lists, and was told to contact this or that organization, where those who answer shout rudely, or disclaim any knowledge of lists and names. How very strange, I tell Lore. Here is money that should be rightfully ours, if indeed our father had paid for life insurance, yet we are prevented from even finding out if we can claim it. And I look at her tattooed arm.

She and the other 199 "Schindler *Juden*" women were not tattooed with a number in Auschwitz, which made them think that soon, very soon, they would be sent to the gas chamber. Lore has a "KL" (*Konzentrationslager*), or concentration camp, tattoo, with which all the slave laborers of the several Mielec camps were marked. I wonder idly whether the German woman who recently photographed tattoo-numbered arms and mounted an exhibition of them knew about the "KL" tattoos. Were "KLs" as interesting to her as numbers? Quite likely not. It is Auschwitz and numbers she was after, not slave labor camps and "KLs." Sometimes people look at Lore's "KL" and ask what it means. Numbers are numbers, I suppose, and need no explaining, but "KL" does. Lore's numberless "KL'd" arm was never even considered for the exhibit because no one would know its meaning. Not quite fair, I think, to overlook the "KLs," some two thousand of them, who built roads for the Baeumer and Loesch company, as Lore did, or worked for the Heinkel aircraft factory. Only a very few survived, among them my sister. Mother saved Lore in 1944 by adding her name to the Schindler list.

When the Russians advanced in the summer of 1944, the slave labor camps were liquidated one by one. First Mother, who had been in Dębica, was sent to Płaszów, where she worked in the office of camp commandant Amon Goeth, who would otherwise be forgotten were it not for the portrayal of this ugly villain in Steven Spielberg's movie *Schindler's List.* Somewhat later, Lore was sent to Płaszów from Cyranka-Berdechow. There may have been a list of new arrivals on which Mother saw her daughter's name. Or she may have seen Lore in the endless prisoner-counting exercises the Germans so liked. After my mother rescued Lore from among the masses of new arrivals, both of them were first shipped to Auschwitz before ending up in Czechoslovakia, thanks to the famous list.

Lore doesn't remember any dates—when she arrived at Płaszów, how long she was there, or when the women were shipped to Auschwitz. For her, the days, weeks, and months merge into one large blur of heat, cold, sun, rain, and mud among thousands of women and their shared misery. Later I learned, and I tell her so, that large numbers of prisoners were brought to Płaszów from liquidated labor camps on February 2, 1944. She and Mother most likely arrived with these. In July 1944, four thousand women were shipped to Stutthof, where they were drowned or shot. Aunt Sheindl and her two daughters perished then. On August 13, 1944, the first transport went to Auschwitz. On September 17, 1944, while the concert season began in Kraków with a piano recital, a large transport of men was shipped to Mauthausen and Auschwitz. On October 15, 1944, two transports left, one for Gross-Rosen, the other for Auschwitz. Uncle Reuven was on the former and he later died in Flossenburg. On October 18, 1944, approximately ten thousand bodies of murdered prisoners were exhumed and burned in Płaszów. Finally, on October 21, 1944, eighteen hundred women and sixteen men were sent to Auschwitz. Among the women were my mother and sister.

Lore and I apply ourselves to the forms in the sunny yard; we read the questions and laugh, as we always do when we would rather cry, but no longer know how. My delicate, beautiful, tattooed, road-gang, slave-laborer sister is about to become an entry in a database. But maybe I am too skeptical. For all I know, a panel of serious gentlemen is already at work deciding how to compensate the slave laborers, what criteria to use. Untold suffering, years irretrievably lost—how will the gentlemen translate them into dollars?

My memory of school is eclipsed by what happened in October 1938. Had I been older or younger, those events in Halle might not have left the strong imprint they did. Although later they would pale in comparison with the terror four years hence, some of the images and details are as vivid now as they were then, the beginning of the first journey.

Father was ill that long-ago October, as he frequently was in fall and winter, with his susceptibility to severe throat infections. It was early evening and already dark, unpleasantly cold outside, a fine drizzle in the air. We were all at home, including Aunt Bekka, each of us occupied with a different task. Father was in bed dozing or reading, I was at the living room table reading or doing homework. Suddenly the doorbell rang loudly and insistently. Then I heard rough male voices in the hallway, and Mother timidly asking questions, and then two or three tall men in shining leather coats stood in the living room. The dim but warm light from the overhead lamp, which I had always liked because of the mysterious shadows it cast in the corners of the room, fell with a very different effect on these leather-coated Germans. These men were not mysterious but threatening, as they stood in the shadows, demanding loudly that we come at once to the police station to verify a formality—yes, all of us, including my sick father, except Aunt Bekka. No need to put on shoes, they said to Father, we had to hurry, he could come in his slippers. It would take only a few minutes. Although we didn't know it at the time, we had to hurry because that night all Polish Jews in Germany and their families had to be found and returned to Poland.

Obediently we put on our coats, while Aunt Bekka stood at the door, wringing her hands, tears running down her face. As if having a premonition, I took a last long look at this room where every family celebration had taken place—the sparkling crystal vases and bowls, the radio with Herzl's blue box above it, Father's desk where he always read the newspaper, the dark wood table with my open books and notebooks. Then we went downstairs.

It was dark and damp outside, the streetlights dim in the chilly drizzle. It seems we walked to the police station, Father in his house slippers. The police station and its jail were brightly lit, as was the cell with bars, a kind of cage actually, into which we were ushered, not altogether impolitely. A number of people were already there, some of them acquaintances of my parents. Since neither chairs nor benches were provided, we prisoners eventually sat down on the floor. Even though the cell was locked, a policeman sat outside, staring at us while we stared at him. New families and single people continued to arrive at regular intervals, until the place became rather crowded. Everyone spoke in whispers, perhaps because we were polite, or because no one wanted the policeman outside the cage to hear. As I recall that night, it is remarkable that no one shouted, wept, or moaned in desperation over having been deposited in a jail cell for no apparent crime. No one got up, clutched the bars, shouted demands or complaints (as prisoners do in movies). Were we not, after all, civilized Jews, even if Polish? All of us in that cell apparently accepted that at one time or another, families, the old and the very young, are picked up in the dark of night and dragged off to brightly lit jails.

The night went on interminably; huddled on the floor of the windowless cell, we didn't know when dawn broke. I don't remember if we were given food or drink. One does not have much of an appetite under these circumstances. At last we were taken to the train station where, under the watchful eyes of policemen, a large crowd milled about on the platform. The train, not yet cattle cars but a civilized passenger train, was waiting. No one saw us off, there were no fond farewells for us, no luggage was handed through the windows and stowed away. There were only grim police in long leather coats watching us board, making sure that not a single Jew escaped. I doubt that it occurred to anyone to do so. And I, a child of not quite nine years of age, knew only what was happening to us, not why.

At last the locomotive whistled once and then twice, as is the custom, and soon Halle was far behind. On and on went the train, without stopping along the way, and Father soon realized that we were going east, to the Polish border. After night fell, Father also realized that the train was not heading to the usual border crossing where, on our visits to the Mielec family in previous years, officials on both sides had inspected passports. And when instead the train came to a halt for the first time, with no station in sight, seemingly in the middle of nowhere, he knew we had been taken to an illegal border crossing. "The green border," said my father—those were his very words. I didn't know at the time that a green border was not a legal and official border with passport control. That it was called green struck me as strange because nothing green was in sight. We got off the train and were standing in a large field that stretched to the far horizon in the pitch-black, moonless night, a vast emptiness with neither houses nor trees. Perhaps it had been green in summer when wheat or potatoes grew there. But at the end of October everything had already been harvested, and all that was left was muddy clay that clung to our shoes and made walking difficult.

Many people were already assembled in the field. Trains must have arrived from other cities earlier, all filled with Polish Jews, who were told now to cross the border and return to Poland. Under the watchful eyes of the German guards we obediently started walking through no-man's-land, but we had not gone very far when we were stopped by Polish border guards. Now a few men from one group, standing close together, deliberated what to do next. A delegation was appointed to explain our situation to the Polish guards. After lengthy negotiations, perhaps due to the rusty Polish of the delegates, they returned to tell us that crossing into Poland was out of the question. We had to go back to Germany. Obediently we turned around, heading back to where we had come from. Now the Germans stopped us and sent us back to the Polish side. Time and again, back and forth we trudged through this muddy no-man's-land between Germany and Poland, pleading to no avail with men on both sides. How bizarre, it seems to me now, a crowd of Polish Jews, many of whom had never even seen Poland, wandering about one dark night in a vast field; nice middle-class, law-abiding citizens, who only two nights earlier had had warm homes, slept in warm beds, but now were dumped onto a muddy field not knowing why, or what would happen to them.

I remember strange things about that long, dark, and cold night. Perhaps it was the wind that was playing tricks with my imagination, perhaps I was hallucinating, adding to and embellishing what I was seeing. I remember a long line of soldiers kneeling on one knee with their guns leveled at us, ready to shoot were we to take one more step. I remember seeing another long line of soldiers wearing helmets and long coats. These men were standing, their guns also pointed at us. We were bound to get shot, it seemed to me, either in front or in back, or from both sides. And then I saw something truly frightening, an apparition of enormous proportions. Far off to one side in a blue policeman's uniform was a man holding a hugely oversized gun. He was so large he seemed to be able to touch the sky. Whereas all of us were in pitch-black darkness, including the lines of soldiers, he was illuminated by a bright light and could be seen very clearly. His great face was not especially threatening, but neither was it kindly. He simply stood there, far away, watching the scene of armed soldiers and the cold and helpless people. Was someone really there, or was it only my imagination?

The night dragged on. We stood. We walked to one side, then the other. We waited. For brief moments I sat under Father's coat to escape the biting wind, and to escape seeing the fearful apparition. Was I afraid of dying during that long, dark night, as I would be in later journeys? I don't think so. Death had not yet shown its fearful face to me. I had not yet heard the screams of the dying.

At dawn the Polish guards finally allowed us to proceed into Poland. I can't remember if it was everyone, or only some of us. During the night we seemed to be part of a very large crowd, but, strangely, by morning only a few of us crossed over. We moved on tired, heavy feet. In the gray dawn, I saw houses here and there surrounded by trees, a welcoming light in their windows. We did not go to these, however, but were led instead to a slaughterhouse. First jail, then a muddy no-man's-land, and then a slaughterhouse— nothing seemed incongruous any longer. Totally exhausted, we collapsed on benches inside the building.

Now there are large gaps in my memory. I don't remember how long we were in the slaughterhouse, or who arranged our departure from it. I didn't think anything dreadful would happen to us, anything like the fate of cows and calves that were brought there, but I don't think I had any coherent thoughts by then. Once more we and those who had been in the slaughterhouse traveled on a train, but unlike in Germany, this train stopped at many stations where Jews with bread, hot tea, and long salamis welcomed us. Having somehow heard of our plight, they handed food through the train windows, smiled encouragement, and called out friendly greetings to the bewildered and disoriented strangers. The train rolled on through harvested fields and villages, and at each station the same scene repeated itself: Strangers handed us food and showed their sympathy, for which we thanked them and shook their hands. Before long we arrived in Mielec.

JANUARY 2000

I search the history books for descriptions of this first, preeminently successful deportation in October 1938 of thousands of Jews and their families, all of whom were considered to be Polish if the family head was a Polish citizen. But I am unable to find much information, not even the exact number of deportees. There may have been fifteen thousand, or twenty thousand, or perhaps only seventeen thousand. One thousand more or less hardly matters to the historian when later he will write about millions.

Long-range economic considerations had a role in the German decision to rid Germany of its Polish Jews. Other reasons may have been closer at hand. One was a Polish order to have the passports of Polish residents abroad stamped at consulates and embassies should they ever wish to return to Poland. It is also possible that the Polish government threatened to cancel passports of its citizens residing abroad. The Nazis might have preferred to rid themselves immediately of thousands of potentially stateless Jews. On the other hand, any excuse would have sufficed to begin the "ethnic cleansing" that for years had been the stated German policy.

Added to the uncertainties of numbers is still another: Were these thousands of people made to cross the border at Zbąszyn, or were several border crossings used? That the circumstances of

this deportation are vague is not surprising. After all, to historians this deportation is an insignificant episode, discussed as no
more than a prelude to Kristallnacht, the pogrom that took place
the following month, when hordes of rampaging Nazis vandal-
ized and burned Jewish properties. Submerged in the more dreadful events of subsequent years is this small beginning of severed
lives, of bank accounts, businesses, and properties lost, of countless families turned overnight into destitute refugees. No lives
were lost, no people shot or beaten to death. As deportations go,
this might be considered a luxury deportation, not really worth
bringing up to today's reader, who has been exposed to more
gruesome fare. And yet, neglecting or ignoring even a portion of
this history puts us in danger of forgetting that, above all, this is
also the history of human lives and human loss. Might it not be
better to remember rather more than too little? For as Y. H.
Yerushalmi tells us, "my terror of forgetting is greater than my
terror of having too much to remember."

We arrived in Mielec laden with salamis and bread. This time we
had no presents for the family, and they had no welcome for us.
We arrived tired and dirty, with neither money nor a change of
clothes. Still, Father's sister, Aunt Feige, and her husband, Uncle
Reuven, made room for us. Grandmother Mindel grumbled, as
was her way—glad, however, to see her only son. She was less
happy to see his family.

In these first weeks in Mielec, life went on somehow. Visitors
came to look at the "refugees," frowned worriedly, and went their
way. Soon my father began to help out in the store, Lore was
apprenticed to a dressmaker (something she sullenly agreed to),
and I quite contentedly began attending the Beit Ya'akov religious school for girls. Mother suffered most. Displaced and disoriented, she silently suffered Grandmother Mindel's hostility

and Aunt Feige's open antagonism. At some point a shipment of a small portion of our belongings arrived—clothes, Mother's jewelry (even Great-grandmother's precious pearls), some books, mattresses, and not much else. These had been packed hastily by Aunt Bekka, who had remained in the flat until the day she sailed for Bolivia wearing an elegant gray silk suit.

Now our situation improved somewhat. We sold those possessions that were not absolutely needed, and our family moved into a two-room flat together with Father's sister Sheindl and her family. Lore became adept at sewing elegant dresses for the local ladies; she was even cheerful and no longer resented her seamstress fate quite as much. The cousins kept close company, including Aunt Feige's daughter Malka. Among Malka's friends was tall Naftule, the baker's son, who doubled as an actor. Mother seemed resigned to the endless chores of shopping, cooking, baking, and laundering. Cousin Püppe scrubbed floors with a vengeance.

Today, looking back at those weeks and months, I am astonished at the speed with which routines were established. Both families, who had lived in large flats of five or more rooms, were reduced to one room each and a shared kitchen. Still, it was as if by common agreement we had switched from one kind of existence to another, as if it were a normal occurrence, as if in the course of one's life a person lived once in one way and then in another. Not that the two families did so with equanimity. The women quarreled. The cousins fought. The kitchen frequently became a battleground. Yet, the eight adults' despair, which they surely must have felt, was well hidden from the child while the seven women and teenagers went about their daily tasks. Meals were cooked, laundry was done, and once a week Mother and I went to the bathhouse, where, under the overhead showers, a dozen or more women of all ages, shapes, and sizes performed their ablutions. Sometimes we luxuriated in steaming bathtubs, which cost more than the showers to use.

Our flat was on the second floor of the Polish landlord's brick house. At the top of the staircase was an open entry used as a work space by whoever was cooking. This led into the small, windowless kitchen with its wood-and-coal cooking range and food cupboard. Next to the kitchen was our relatives' room with its balcony, and one crossed their room to reach a door that opened on ours. The rooms were small, crowded as they were with beds: We had two single beds and at night a foldaway bed was added. The question of who had to sleep with whom often led to prolonged arguments. Next to our room was a small attic to which I often escaped when I wanted to be alone, when I felt I needed to have my own space in this crowd of people. Through the grimy attic window I watched the yard, the people who came and went, the tenants who drew water from the well or hung out laundry. I wanted to believe then that no one knew where I was, although I cannot really explain why that was important. I wanted to watch the others while they didn't think themselves watched.

How was it that I adjusted so easily, almost effortlessly, to this new existence? I might have, as it were, changed from one kind of personality to another, learned to play a role as actors do. Or did I merely pretend, as I would later pretend to be Polish? I don't think so. Finding my place, my home, was much more genuine, more real and natural, like the chrysalis that changes effortlessly into the insect it is destined briefly to be. From the spoiled, well-mannered Jewish-German girl I changed in no time into an assertive Jewish-Polish youngster. Without making a special effort, I soon read and spoke Yiddish with my schoolmates, read Polish books, and played hide-and-go-seek with Esther, Tova, and their friends in the dark alleys of our neighborhood. Fervently, as if I had done so all my life, I said the morning prayers each day, while Father smiled quiet approval and Mother looked puzzled. She was religious in her own way, observant though not given to piety. My turn to the religious life may have struck her as more appropriate for a boy.

Without a backward glance at the Halle past, I made myself at home in the Mielec present. I longed neither for the books and toys I once had, nor for my mother's special foods. I didn't even miss the aunts, uncles, and cousins of Mother's large family. They belonged to a world from which I was expelled and which for me had ceased to exist, especially because, as the months went by, I knew that that family too had left that world, had gone to exotic-sounding places such as Bolivia and Argentina. Halle was no more than a desolate barren landscape, no longer peopled by those I once knew. "Gone and ended those times, empty and distant, like something within a dream," wrote the poet-king Li Yü after losing his kingdom, to which, he knew, he would never return. Although my father's Polish family was not especially fond of me, nor I of them, and Cousin Esther and I quarreled incessantly, I was now at home. Neither then, nor ever again thereafter, did I wish to see the place where I was born and where my family, I later realized, had all along been unwelcome strangers. Paradoxically, in Mielec, we were not. Could I as a child have sensed this unspoken truth?

Mielec was home for me as no other home would ever be. This was my father's home and the home of his father's father before him; here neither he nor I was a stranger. After Mielec all other homes were merely places for me, the sojourner's impermanent rest. The times of rest might be longer or shorter; the stranger might be less or more welcome, connected or not to the place and its people. Yet no place or way station would ever belong to me or I to it other than Mielec, where this, the first journey, had ended for too brief a time.

POSTSCRIPT

Transforming remembered multidimensional scenes charged with emotions, imbued with sounds and half-remembered smells, and seen by the inner eye as movements and color, into words flattened onto paper is ultimately unsatisfactory. Nor can one be, in the final analysis, satisfied with the depiction of the many faces of fear, anguish, the sorrow of loss, or the estrangement felt when returning to the world where displacements were only partial or had not occurred. Wallace Fowlie, in considering the writing of autobiography, notes a "curious escape from life into words, this leap from an intention . . . to the expression of the intention," which leads to a sense of foolishness. It is not only foolishness, I would add, but also inevitable dismay at the inadequacy of words, their shortcomings when compared to the intensity of the memory they are meant to convey.

The task of the historian is to rescue from oblivion, to document, to explain, to find meaning, to make sense of portions of the past. And while I have attempted as faithfully and as honestly as I could to preserve and document a small fragment, the destruction of Jewish Mielec and its people, I am at a loss where meaning or sense is concerned. A changing and evolving culture, a tradition—call it Yiddish culture, together with its guardians and those who perpetuated it—was destroyed, rooted out. To be sure, today a building here or there, a cemetery, a synagogue, remnants and reminders, might be renovated and, a plaque affixed, become a tourist attraction. But all such restoration and making presentable is, in effect, "museumification"; the life that was has become a museum piece. Instead of a living, changing culture we have lifeless museums and exhibits in glass cases with neat labels attached.

We also have the re-created Holocaust with the latest technology in Holocaust centers. The proliferation of such centers in American cities is astounding. No longer mere museums with presumably boring exhibits, some of these centers are firmly lodged in the computer age, where the visitor is not a spectator but is required to participate, as if in a video game, in a simulation game of the Holocaust. They, however, also want to show "the real thing," whether it is a nicely refurbished Polish cattle car or paving stones from the Warsaw ghetto or death masks of beheaded Jewish prisoners that had been ordered by the Vienna Museum of Natural History during the Nazi period.

Joseph R. Levenson reminds us that "preserving the past by recounting it, or displaying its bequests, is not perpetuating it." And he tells the story of the Baal Shem, who, when confronted by a difficult task, went to a certain place in the forest, lit a fire, and prayed, and his task was accomplished. A generation later, the place in the forest and the prayers were still known, and in the generation thereafter only the place in the forest was remembered. But in the generation of Rabbi Israel of Rizhin, the place, how to light the fire, and how to say the prayer were forgotten. All he could do was tell the story.

But are the stories museums tell enough? Should we congratulate ourselves for having labels on glass cases, plaques on buildings, and even monuments? We need these in order to remember, goes the argument. Yet, how much are we forgetting while we remember? And exactly what is it that we remember when we leave a Holocaust center, aside from its technological perfection?

By attempting to translate life into words, I fear that I too have contributed to forgetting. I have, inevitably, left so much out. And as at the beginning of this writing so now at its end, the meaning of wanton destruction continues to elude me. To me, my words seem hollow. Sadly I agree with the Chinese poet who wrote this couplet a long time ago:

Always dissatisfaction remains when the end is reached
—dare we then be complacent and cherish our conceit?

NOTES

ONE FIRST JOURNEYS

4 EIGHT THOUSAND JEWS: Due to the influx of refugees, it is impossible to establish how many Jews were in Mielec at the beginning of 1942. See Mark Verstandig, *I Rest My Case,* trans. Felicity Verstandig (Melbourne: Melbourne University Press, 1997), pp. 138–139; he estimates the number of Jews expelled from Mielec at ten thousand. This figure seems too high, considering that the Jewish population numbered around five thousand in 1939. It is not clear why the German document quoted on page 10 gives a figure of 4,500. This figure may be inaccurate, or it may reflect the fact that only that many Jews were sent to the Lublin district, the rest being killed or selected for work.

6 OPERATION REINHARD: Trial Record, Freiburg, 206 AR376/63, in Yad Vashem Archives, TR-10/607. Operation Reinhard was a special organization launched in autumn 1941, *before* the Wannsee Conference of January 1942. It was headed by the SS and police leader Odilo Globocnik.

6 GENERAL GOVERNMENT OF POLAND: The Generalgouvernement. It was established in October 1939 and consisted of those areas that were not incorporated into Germany.

6 "FROM THE HALLWAY": Josef Kermisz, ed., *Dokumenty i materiały do dziejów okupacji Niemieckiej w Polsce* (Documents and materials regarding the events of the German occupation of Poland) (Łódź: Centralna Żydowska Komisja Historyczna w Polsce, 1946), p. 12. My translation.

10 "NEW NUMBER IS 4,500": See note to page 4, above.

10 *VOLKSDEUTSCHER:* One of the ethnic Germans who lived outside Germany proper. They gave overwhelming support to the

German occupiers; the men joined the SS and local branches of the Gestapo.

13 "IN THE LUBLIN DISTRICT": Philip Friedman, *Roads to Extinction: Essays on the Holocaust,* ed. Ada June Friedman (New York and Philadelphia: Conference on Jewish Social Studies, Jewish Publication Society of America, 1980), p. 227.

14 (*"IN EINEM BLUTRAUSCH"*): Trial Record, Freiburg, AR 376/63, in Yad Vashem Archives, TR-10/1161Z, vol. 3. My translation.

17 "12 O'CLOCK NOON": Kermisz, *Dokumenty i materiały,* p. 24. My translation.

18 "NO DIFFICULTIES DURING SHIPPING": Ibid., p. 29. My translation.

21 RETURN TO THE GENERAL GOVERNMENT: Ibid., p. 33. My translation.

21 IN JULY 1942: The path of murder by this battalion is documented in Christopher R. Browning, *Ordinary Men: Reserve Police Battalion 101 and the Final Solution in Poland* (New York: HarperCollins, 1992).

24 PICTURE ON A SUKKAH WALL: A sukkah, literally "booth," was built under the open sky for Sukkoth, the Jewish autumn harvest festival, by householders. Meals were usually eaten in the booth. It was customary to decorate the booth with harvested fruit and pictures, including a picture of Jerusalem.

TWO MORE JOURNEYS

25 "DISPERSE THROUGHOUT THE COUNTRYSIDE": Kermisz, *Dokumenty i materiały,* p. 11.

32 "PROPERTIED JEWS IS MANDATORY": Werner Praeg and W. Jacobmeyer, eds., *Das Diensttagebuch des deutschen Generalgouverneurs in Polen 1939–1945* (The official diary of the German General Governor in Poland 1939–1945) (Stuttgart: Deutsche Verlagsanstalt, 1975), p. 512. My translation.

32 WITH THEIR OWN MONEY: Information supplied by a former inmate of the Cyranka-Berdechow camp.

51 BECOMING GERMAN CITIZENS: Poznań (Posen) was incorporated into Germany after September 1939 and the population was required to become German. Those who wanted to remain Polish citizens left.

THREE WHEN GRANDMOTHER DIED

55   A GRAY ONE ON THE SABBATH: At marriage Jewish women shaved
their heads and wore wigs, though some wore only kerchiefs.
Women who kept their hair and did not cover it were considered
modern. Being modern did not mean, however, that they ceased
to maintain Jewish observances. Modernity arrived in small-town
Poland incrementally and through selectively adopted changes.

59   NEVILLE CHAMBERLAIN: Chamberlain (1869–1940) was responsible for the policy of appeasing Hitler in Munich in 1938, which led
to the German occupation of Czechoslovakia.

70   "EXHAUSTED" OR "FEEBLE": Kabbalah, meaning "tradition," is the
mystic branch of Judaism, but "Kabbalists" is a popular catch-
word for mystics of all kinds. The numerological game referred to
here is based on the fact that the Hebrew letters of the alphabet
also represent numbers. In this instance Adolf = 121, Hitler = 324,
and Mielec = 260 make the sum total of 705. Each of the numbers,
7, 0, and 5, in turn, can be written also with a Hebrew letter of the
alphabet. When the three letters are formed into a word, *tashah,*
which means "exhausted" or "feeble," results. And since the letters
of the alphabet are also used to indicate the year, *tashah* is 1945.

71   READING *THE DREAM OF THE RED CHAMBER*: *The Dream of the
Red Chamber* (Hong lou meng), also called *The Story of the Stone,*
appeared in its first printed edition in 1792. The author, Cao Xue-
qin (1715?–1763), died before completing the book and Gao Ê
(1749?–1815) added the last forty chapters to the 120-chapter
edition we have today. An excellent translation in five volumes is
The Story of the Stone, trans. David Hawkes (New York: Penguin
Books, 1973–1986).

72   REGISTERS OF THEIR LIVES: Chapter 5 of the novel relates Baoyu's
dream visit to the fairy world with its bureaucratic organization
much like that of today's world. Registers that record the past,
present, and future of all the world's girls are kept in the fairy
world.

77   "BURNED ALIVE IN THE SYNAGOGUE": Martin Gilbert, *The Holocaust: The Jewish Tragedy* (London: Collins, 1986), p. 87.

77   "ALL DIED": Feliks Kiryka, ed., *Mielec, Dzieje miasta i regionu*
(Mielec, events of the town and region) (Rzeszów: Krajowa Agen-
cja Wydawnicza, 1984), vol. 2, p. 219.

78 WHEN HE LEARNED OF THE SS DOINGS: See Walter Goerlitz, "Reichenau: Field Marshal Walter von Reichenau," in *Hitler's Generals,* ed. Correlli Barnett (London: Weidenfeld & Nicolson, 1989), p. 214.

81 FEAST OF TABERNACLES: Known also as Sukkoth, it follows the New Year (Rosh Hashanah) and the Day of Atonement (Yom Kippur) and was originally a harvest festival. During Sukkoth, which lasts seven days, families are supposed to eat and spend as much time as possible in an impermanent structure, a booth (*sukkah*), with a roof of tree branches through which the sky can be seen.

82 "CONSULATE IN GERMANY": T. Berenstein, et al., comps., eds., *Eksterminacja Żydów na ziemiach Polskich, w okresie okupacji hitlerowskiej* (The extermination of Jews on Polish soil during Hitler's occupation) (Warszawa: Żydowski Instytut Historyczny w Polsce, 1957), pp. 55–56.

FOUR TOŚKA

100 "POLISH AND JEWISH CUSTOMERS": Verstandig, *I Rest My Case,* pp. 114, 119–120.

101 THE ONSET OF WINTER: Here memory fails me. All I remember is that our clandestine school existed during the cold weather. We may have begun lessons in the fall of 1940 and stopped before the start of spring in 1941. I also cannot recall how many months we actually attended school; it may have been only three months in autumn 1941. By January 1942, when the deportation from Mielec threatened, we would certainly not have attended school any longer.

104 NOT TRAVELLED MORE: Edna St. Vincent Millay, "The Unexplorer," in *Collected Lyrics of Edna St. Vincent Millay* (New York: Harper & Brothers, 1943).

FIVE SOUP KITCHENS AND TAPESTRIES

124 COVERED THE ROOF WITH SHEETING: The Polish dictation is in my diary, which I kept from 1945 to 1947. The diary is a tattered gray notebook, which I first used briefly for school exercises in Poznań. In it I also kept poems collected along the way, or those that I wrote.

128 OSKAR SCHINDLER: Oskar Schindler (1908–1974) was an ethnic German from what is now Moravia in the Czech Republic. His controversial personality—shrewd businessman, hard-drinking, fast-living—is captured supremely well in the book by Thomas Keneally, *Schindler's List* (New York: Simon and Schuster, 1982), on which Steven Spielberg's 1993 movie is based. In October 1944, Schindler managed to requisition over one thousand Jews (a list of their names was compiled) who had worked in his Kraków factory for his more or less fictitious factory in Brünlitz. Schindler died in Germany and is buried in the Latin Cemetery of Jerusalem.

134 NOVELS BY HENRYK SIENKIEWICZ: Sienkiewicz (1846–1916) was a major Polish novelist. His best-known novel is *Quo Vadis?* Published in 1896, it was translated into more than thirty languages.

139 RETURNED TO POLAND IN 1961: Jerzy Szablowski, ed., *The Flemish Tapestries at Wawel Castle in Kraków: Treasures of King Sigismund Augustus Jagiello* (Antwerp: Fond Mercator, 1972), pp. 67–69. Aubusson was once famed for its tapestry manufacture. Unfortunately, there is no indication as to who loaded the Wawel treasures on the barge for the journey down the Vistula.

SIX CHOICES

144 THE KARLOV CAMP: According to Yehuda Bauer, *Flight and Rescue: Brichah* (New York: Random House, 1970), p. 109, the Karlov camp at Pilsen was set up as a transit point at the beginning of July 1945.

154 AN EDITORIAL ABOUT US: Arno Rudert, *"Hans und Lore,"* *Frankfurter Rundschau*, no. 18, September 19, 1945, is an editorial using our family's experiences to advocate that Germany become democratic.

157 THEOLOGIANS AND EDUCATORS TODAY: Eli Wohlgelernter, "Once Again Where Was God?" *Jerusalem Post*, May 5, 2000, discusses a conference held in Ashkelon, "The Impact of the Holocaust on Jewish Theology and Thought," where the question was raised.

158 "IN LIFE'S LARGE GLASS": The poem, in German, has no indication of author or date, and I assume it is mine.

161 THIS FRIENDSHIP POETRY: The poems by Wei Yingwu (736–830?), Wang Wei (699–759), and Du Fu (712–770) were translated from

the anthology *Xinyi Tang shi sanbei shou* (New interpretations of Three Hundred Tang Poems) (Taibei: Sanmin Shuju, 1976), pp. 39, 324, 14–15.

164 BETWEEN THE CAMP AND UNRRA: The United Nations Relief and Rehabilitation Administration was replaced in 1947 by IRO, the International Refugee Organization.

168 IN JANUARY 1946: *"Di Konferenz fun di befrajte Yidn in der Amerikaner Zone"* (The conference of liberated Jews in the American Zone), *Dos Fraje Vort,* no. 18, February 1946. The paper was published in Feldafing in Latin-alphabet transcription.

169 *HEINRICH HEINE:* The German-Jewish poet (1797 or 1799–1856) was baptized in 1825. An invalid for the last nine years of his life, he returned to the grandeur of the Hebrew scriptures during his infirmity.

169 KAROL SZPALSKI: After these many years I no longer know why I wrote Szpalski, Szpilman as the author of this poem. Although I have not been able to locate the poem in the anthologies and encyclopedias available to me, I am quite certain that, as stated in the text, the author is Karol Szpalski (1908–1963), well-known writer and poet, including satiric poetry. I thank David Weinfeld for information about Szpalski.

171 MADE MUCH SENSE TO ME: These poems by Christian Morgenstern (1871–1914) I probably read in Morgenstern, *Alle Galgenlieder* (Berlin: Verlag Bruno Cassirer, 1935).

174 HAVING BOARDED THE *MARINE PERCH:* The *Marine Perch* was a troopship chartered for passenger service in 1946 with 920 accommodations. See Frederick E. Emmons, *American Passenger Ships: The Ocean Lines and Liners, 1873–1983* (Newark: University of Delaware Press, 1985), p. 36.

176–177 AS HANNA KRALL WROTE: Krall's short story is in her *Taniec na cudzym weselu* (Dancing at another wedding) (Warsaw: Polska Oficyna Wydawnicza BGW, 1993), pp. 131–174.

SEVEN IN THE BEGINNING

179 Trude Maurer, "The Background for Kristallnacht: The Expulsion of Polish Jews," in Walter H. Pehle, ed., *November 1938, From 'Reichskristallnacht' to Genocide* (New York and Oxford: Berg Publishers, Inc., 1991), pp. 44–72.

183 MANUFACTURED FEATHERBEDDING: Details about Mielec are
from Keitelman, *"Di Yiddishe kehile in Melic"* (The Jewish community in Mielec), in *Fun noentn ovar* (The recent past) (New York:
CYCO–Bicher Farlag, 1955), pp. 401–451. The six grain dealers are
listed in *The Galician Business Directory.*

189 "A BROKEN SHARD OF THE PAST": Stephen Owen, *Remembrances:
The Experience of the Past in Classical Chinese Literature* (Cam-
bridge, Mass.: Harvard University Press, 1986), p. 102.

198 PUBLICIZING THE LISTS: Among a number of articles that have
appeared in the American and Jewish-American press about the
insurance companies' reluctance to publish names of policyhold-
ers, Si Frumkin's comments on this topic in the *Los Angeles Times,*
May 11, 2000, are especially perceptive.

199 MOUNTED AN EXHIBITION: The photographic exhibit of tattooed
arms is in Andreas Kuhne, *"Die sichtbaren Zeichen des Schreck-
ens"* (The visible signs of dread), *Süddeutsche Zeitung,* October 26,
1999. I thank Professor Knut Walf for bringing this article to my
attention.

199 SOME TWO THOUSAND OF THEM: The figure of two thousand slave
laborers in the Mielec camps is in Frank Golczewski, *"Polen,"* in
Wolfgang Benz, ed., *Dimension des Völkermords: Die Zahl der
jüdischen Opfer des Nationalsozialismus* (Dimension of national
murder: The number of Jewish victims of National Socialism)
(Munich: R. Oldenbourg, 1991), p. 144.

200 SENT TO AUSCHWITZ: The chronology is according to Tadeusz
Wronski, *Kronika okupowanego Krakowa* (Chronicle of Occupied
Kraków) (Kraków: Wydawnictwo Literackie, 1974), pp. 322, 358–
360, 372–373.

207 "TOO MUCH TO REMEMBER": Yosef Hayim Yerushalmi, *Zakhor:
Jewish History and Jewish Memory* (New York: Schocken Books,
1989), p. 117.

210 "WITHIN A DREAM": The line of poetry is from Li Yü (937–978),
"Song of the Night's Third Watch."

POSTSCRIPT

212 "EXPRESSION OF THE INTENTION": Wallace Fowlie, "On Writing
Autobiography," in James Olney, ed., *Studies in Autobiography*
(New York: Oxford University Press, 1988), p. 165.

213 BEHEADED JEWISH PRISONERS: The death mask exhibit was re-
     ported by Mariam Niroumand, *Die Tageszeitung,* August 7, 1997,
     p. 10. I thank Professor Knut Walf for bringing this item to my
     attention.

213 TELLS THE STORY: Retold according to Gershom Scholem's
     version. Joseph R. Levenson, *Confucian China and Its Modern
     Fate: A Trilogy* (Berkeley: University of California Press, 1968),
     pp. 124–125. Martin Buber has a slightly different version of this
     story. See his *Tales of the Hasidim: The Later Masters* (New York:
     Schocken Books, 1948), pp. 92–93.

214 "CHERISH OUR CONCEIT": The couplet was translated by E. R.
     Hughes, in *The Art of Letters: Lu Chi's "Wen Fu," A.D. 302* (New
     York: Pantheon, 1951), p. 106.

ACKNOWLEDGMENTS

Were it not for my good friends Harold R. Isaacs and his wife, Viola, the writing of this story would have never begun. They were the ones who told me to start, and I sorrowfully regret that they did not live to see its end. Nor would these pages have been completed without Barbara C. Johnson's unflagging encouragement. The precious friendship and support of these three people led to the first products of this enterprise when, a number of years ago, I published three fictionalized short stories. But in the end the fictional format proved unsatisfactory, and there began a long period of writing and rewriting, mainly during sabbatical leaves from the Hebrew University of Jerusalem. I am grateful to my friends and colleagues who, in the course of these years, read portions of the manuscript and gave me the benefit of their invaluable comments. I deeply appreciate Andrew Ramer's perceptive responses and the sensitive insights and comments by Felicity Bloch, Shalom Eilati, Ami Elad, Joan Hill, Avraham Altman, Cecile Panzer, Yoav and Raya Ariel, and Rita and Alexandre Blumstein. Barbara Johnson's critical reading at various stages of writing and finally of the entire text was enormously helpful. Uri Melammed guided me through the intricacies of numerology and Miriam Isaacs saved me from committing grave errors in Yiddish transcription. I also must thank Wolfgang Kubin and David Shipler for their ongoing interest in this project and their support. My sister, Lore Smith, and my daughter, Miriam Eber, bravely read each chapter I sent to them and cheered me on. Due especially to Miriam's computer expertise the old photographs were readied for this publication. To Nicole Morris I owe a special debt of gratitude: Her critical eye and thorough and sensitive reading of all the chapters were invaluable in helping me see where time and again I had gone astray. Philippa Bacal expertly coped with the intricacies of computer technology. Finally, special thanks are due Jonathan Segal, my editor, whose patience and endurance I deeply admire, and Ida Giragossian, who graciously coped with my questions. That shortcomings remain is due to my own imperfections.

INDEX